HALLOWEEN

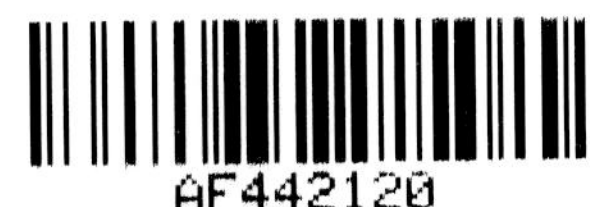

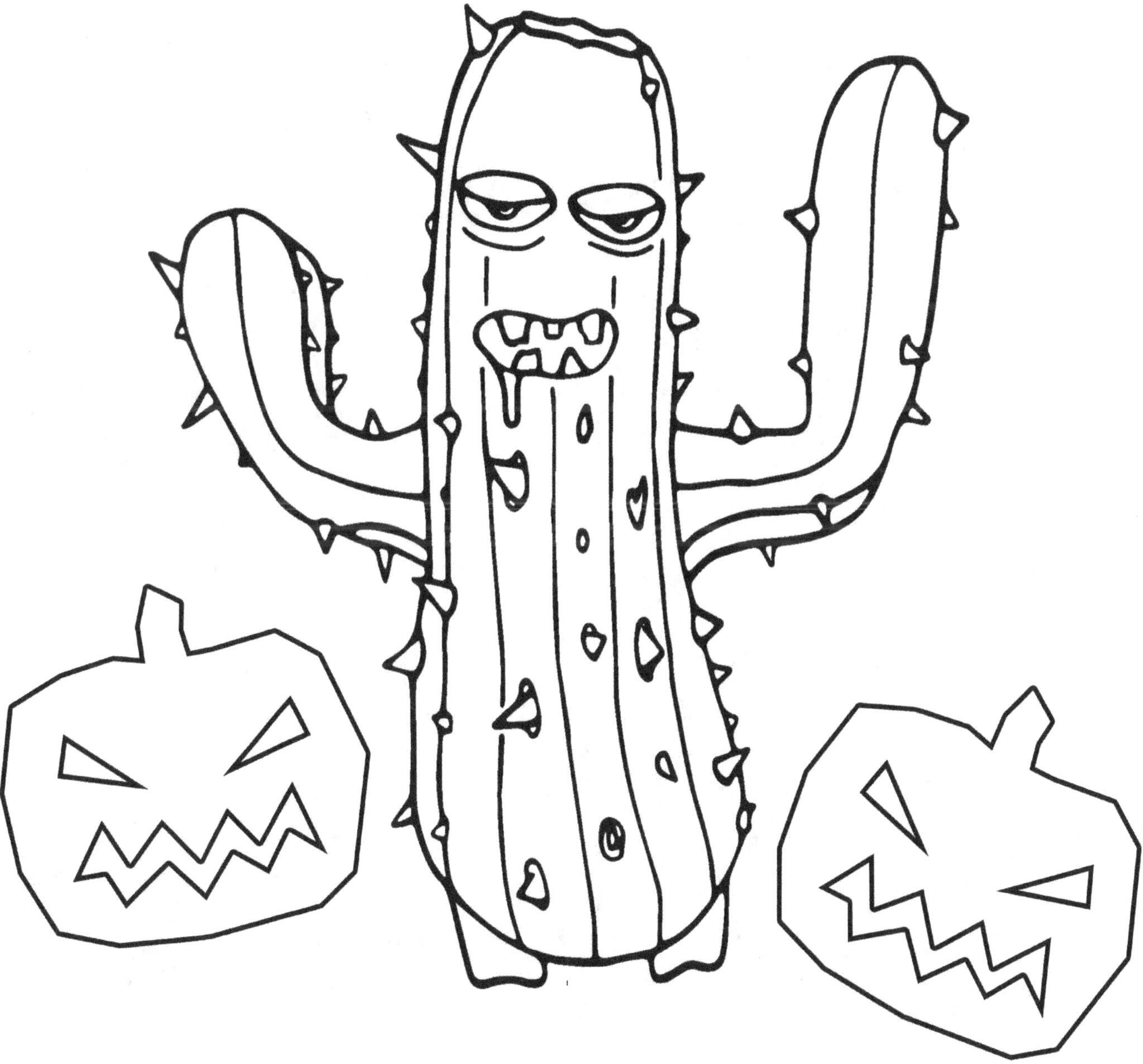

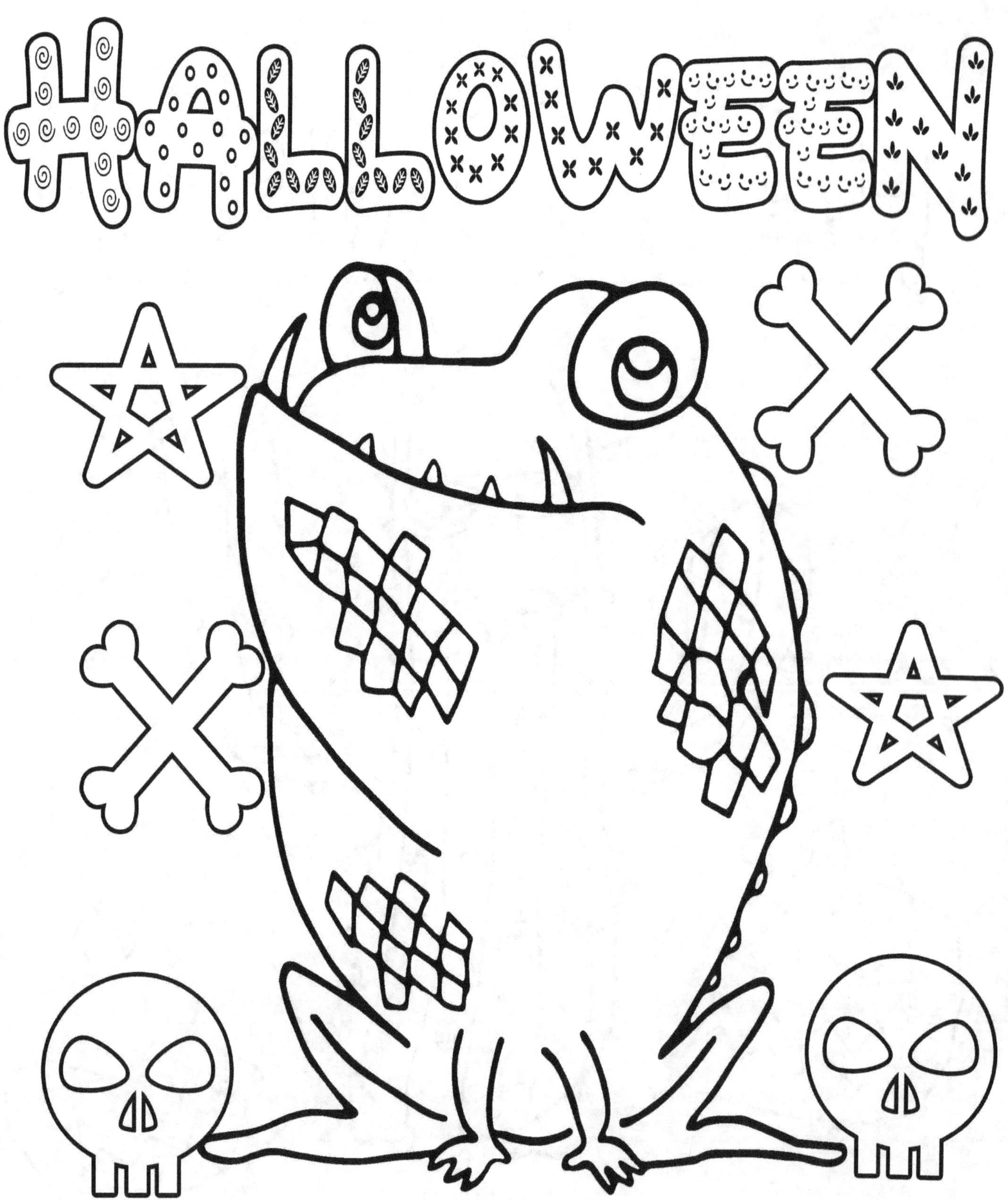

HALLOWEEN

SPOOKY

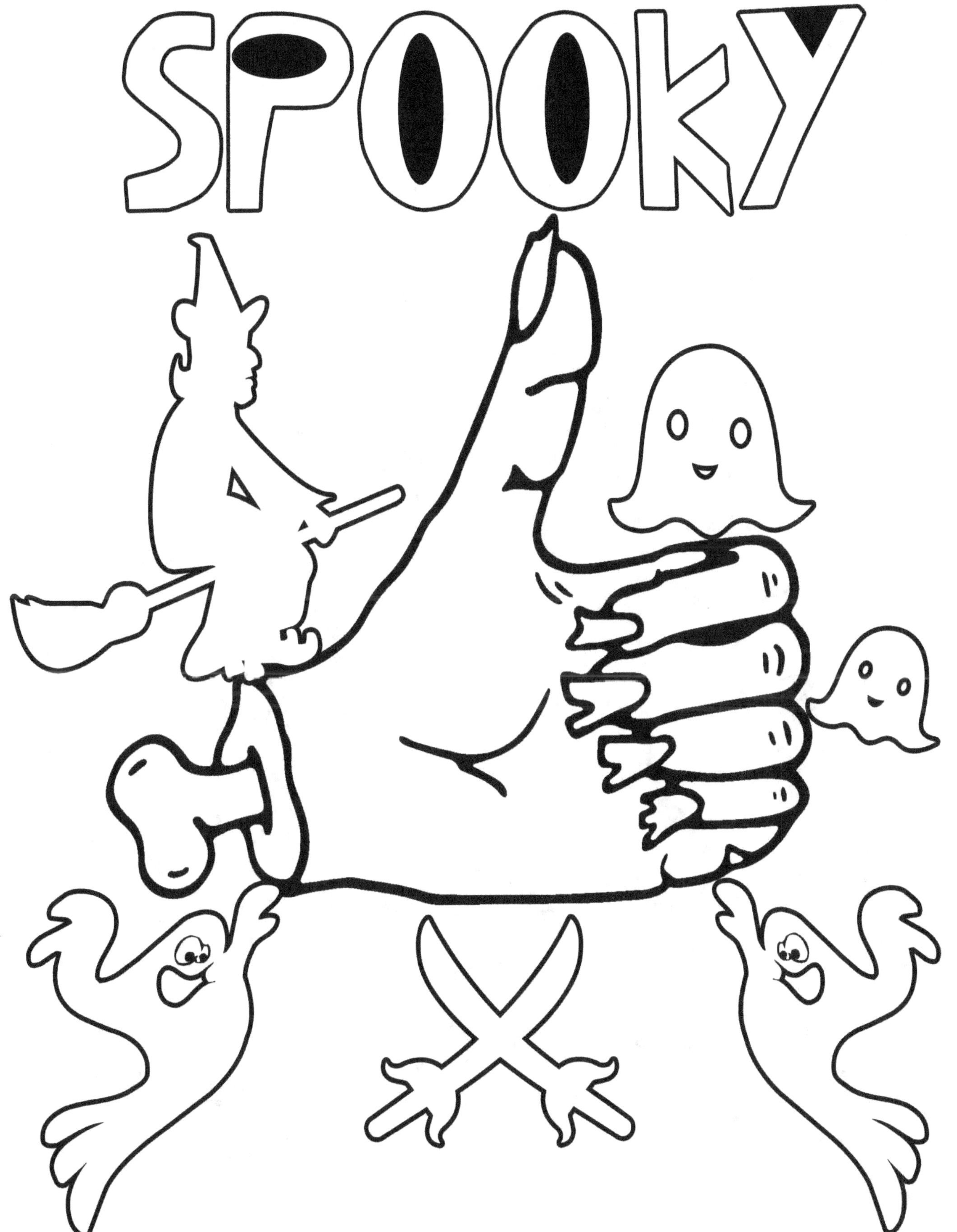

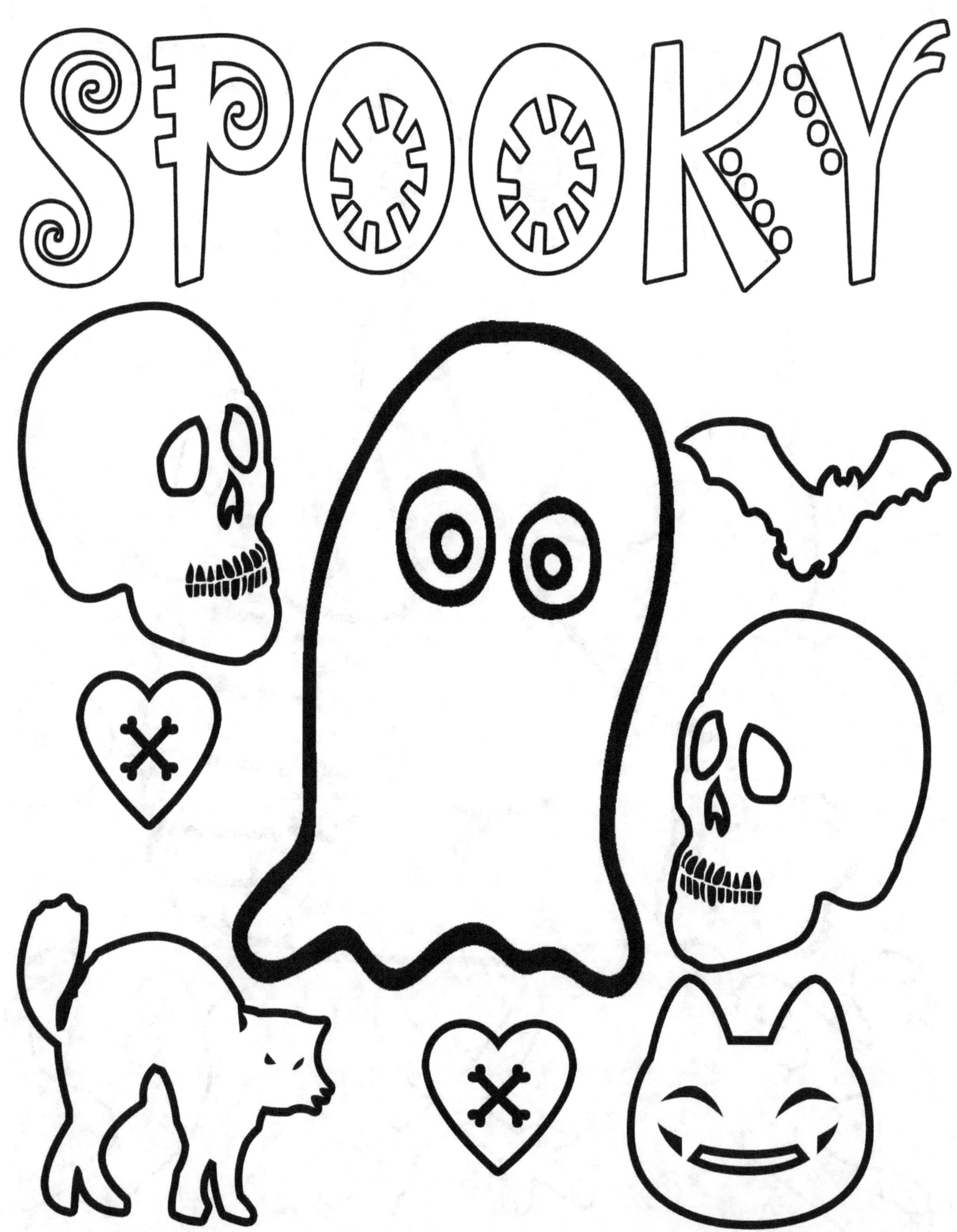

SPOOKY

HORROR

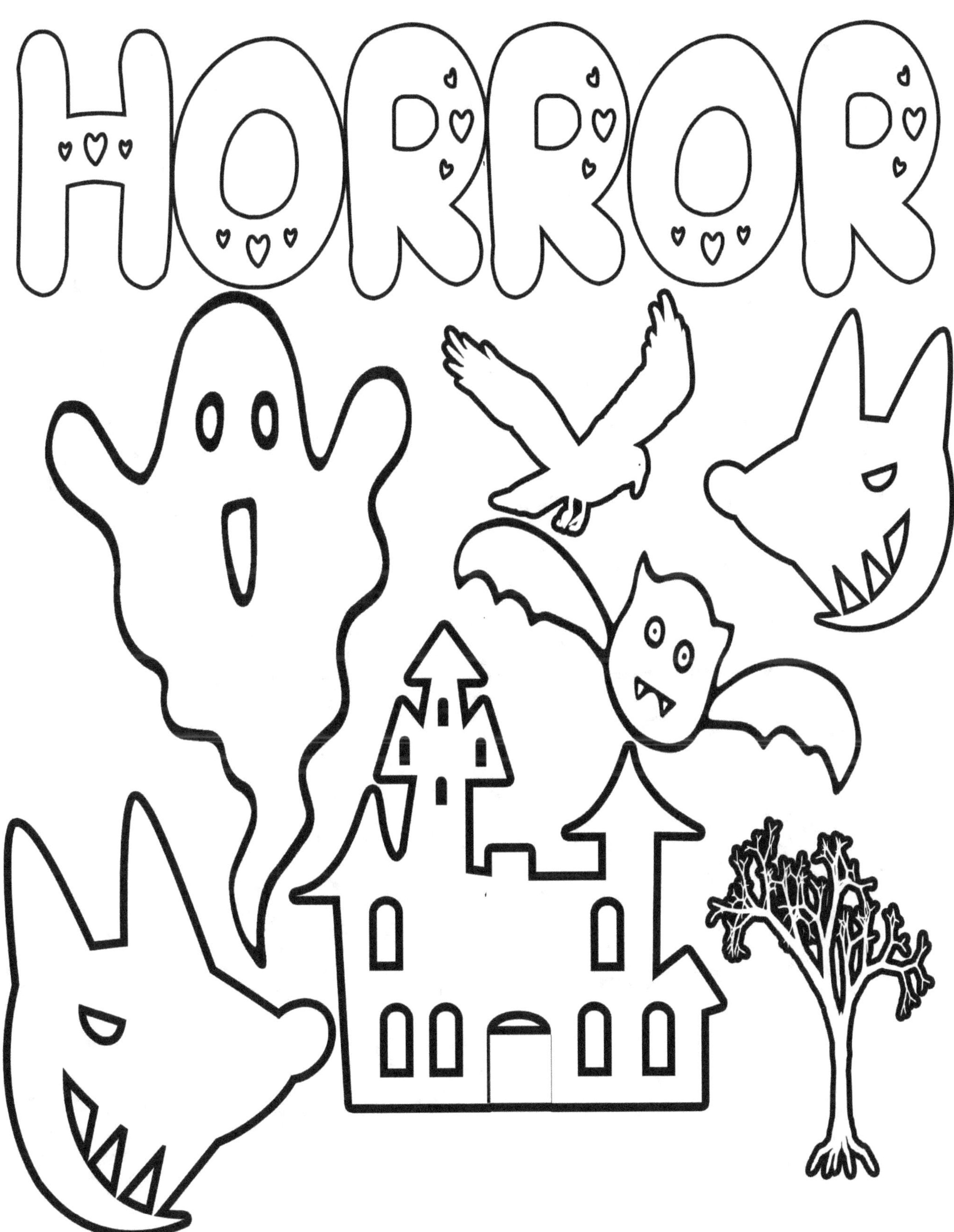

HORROR

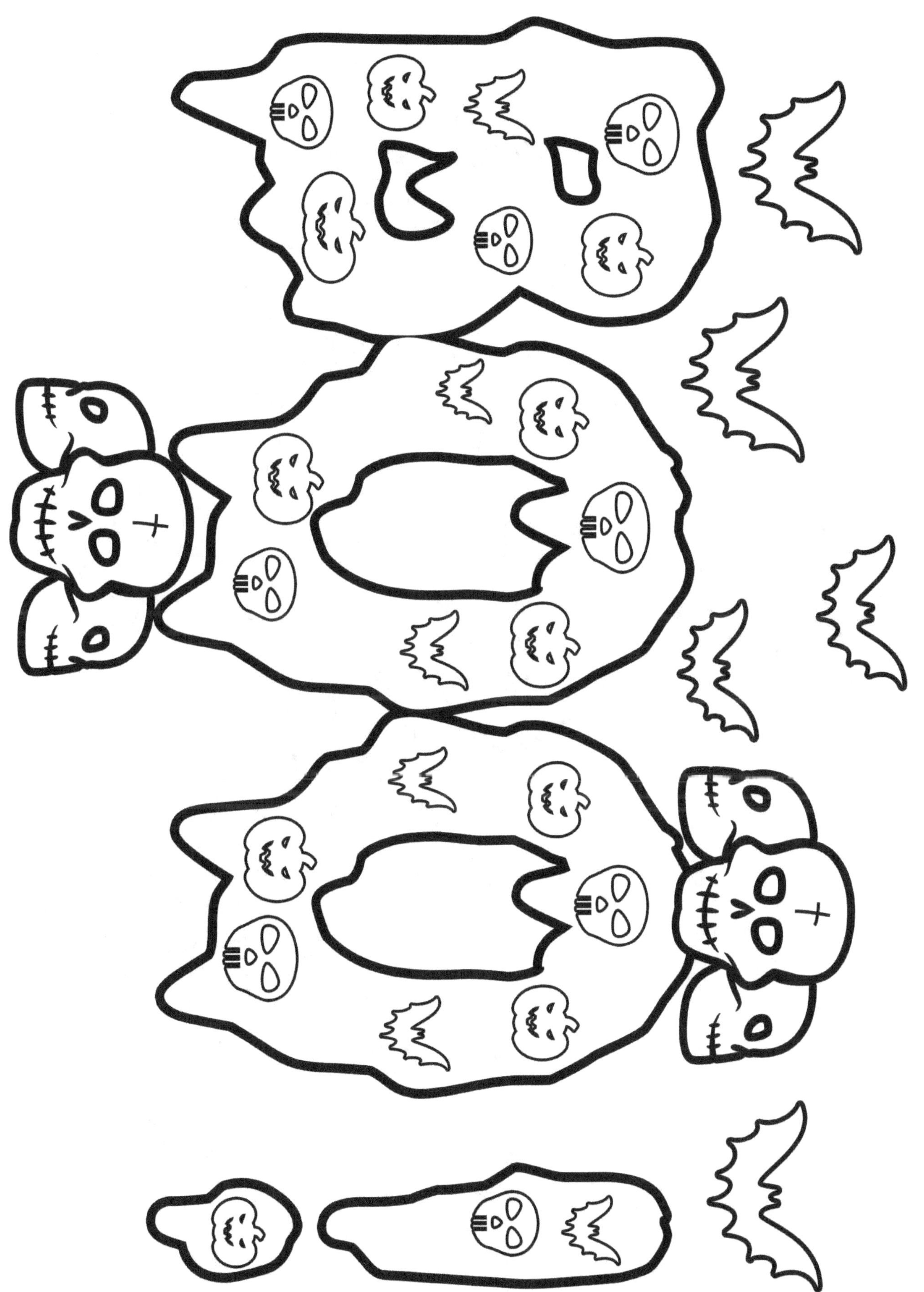

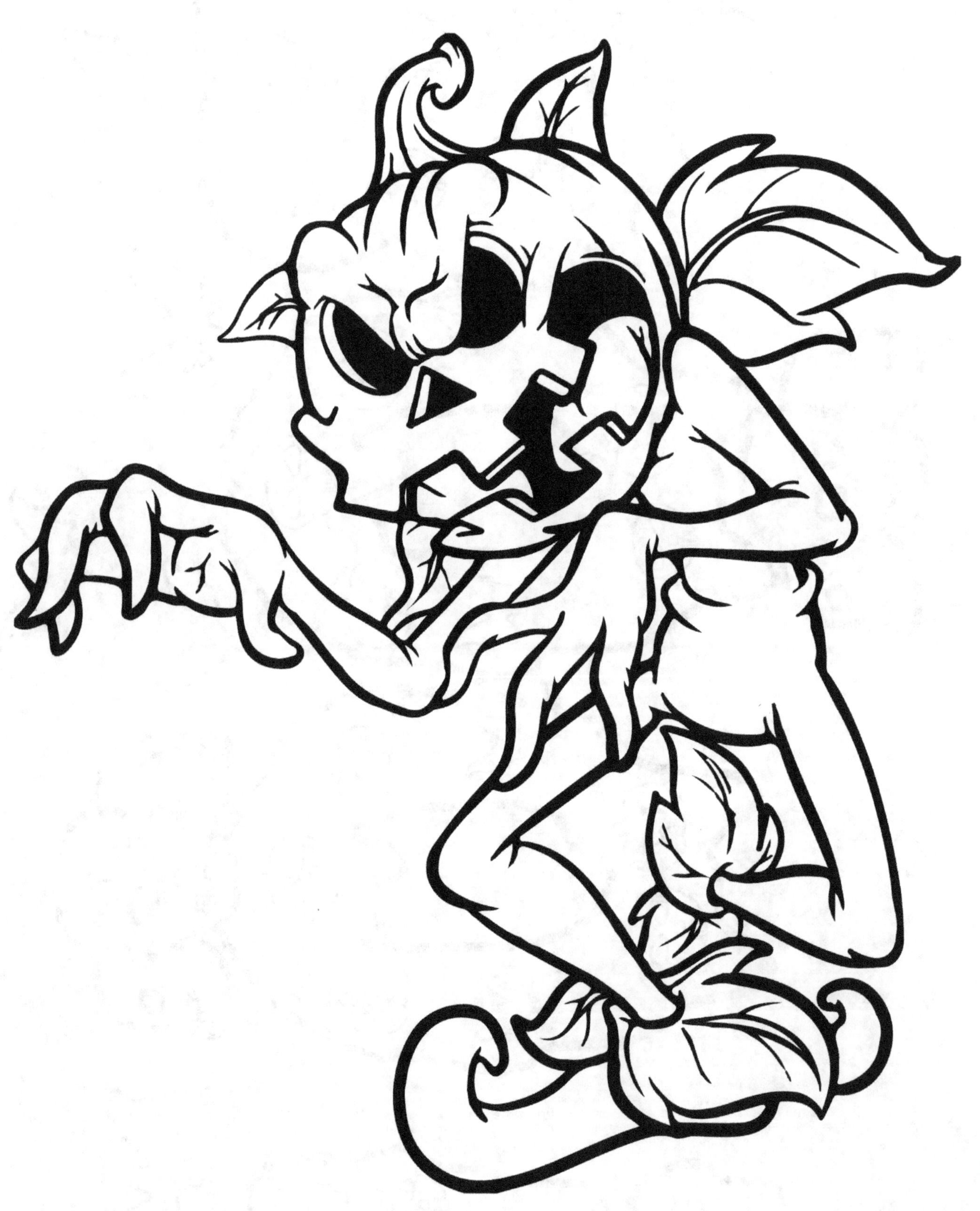

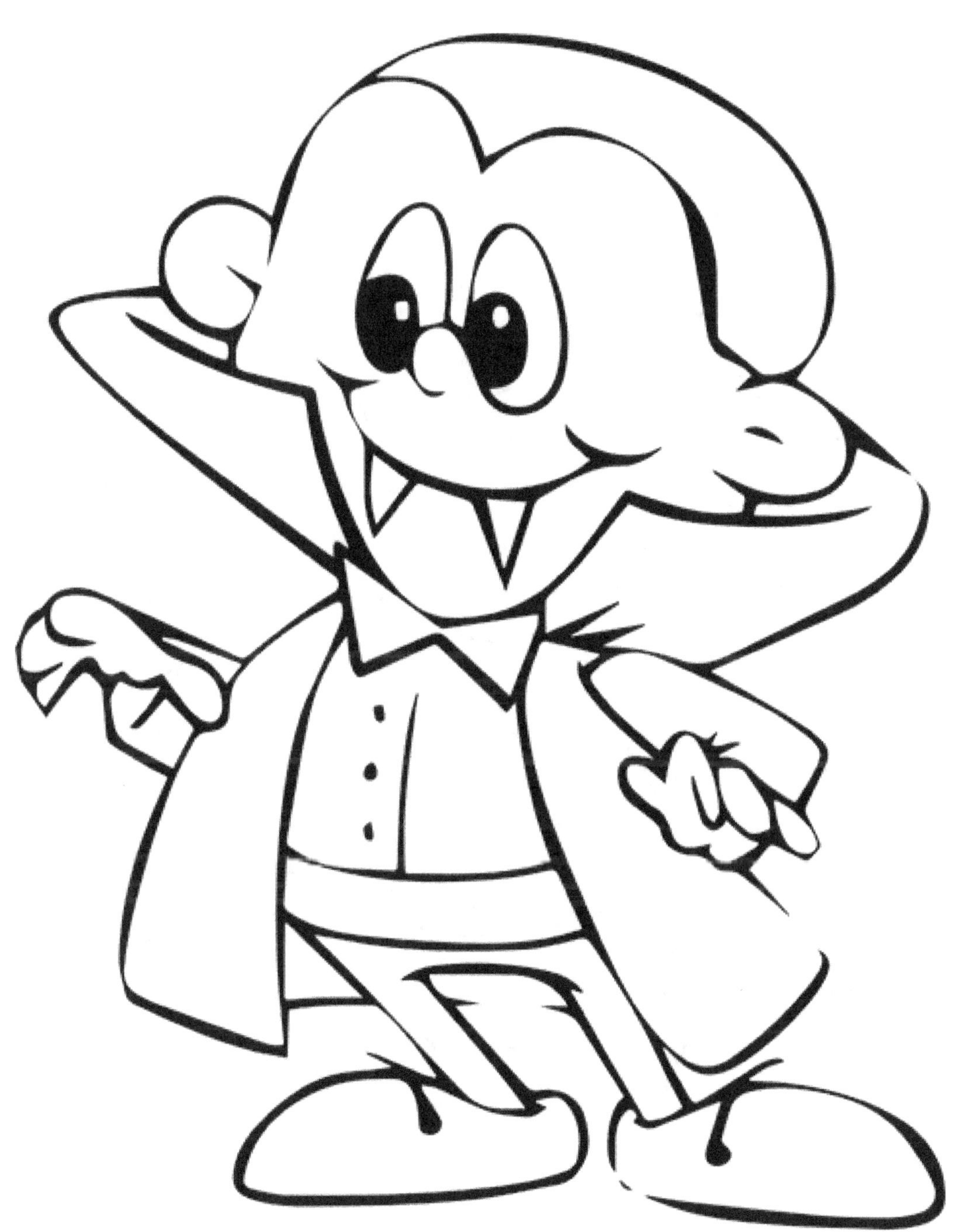

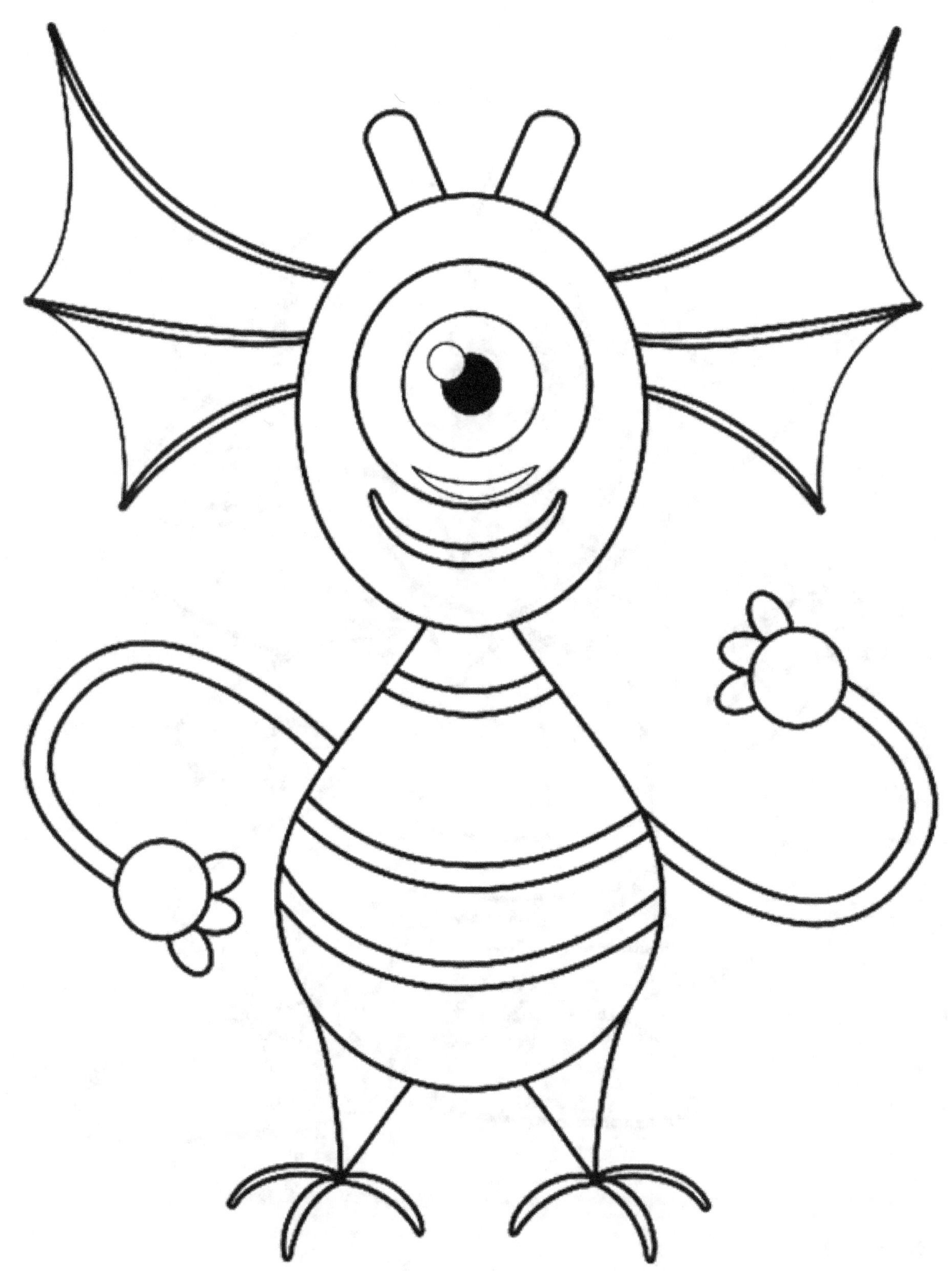

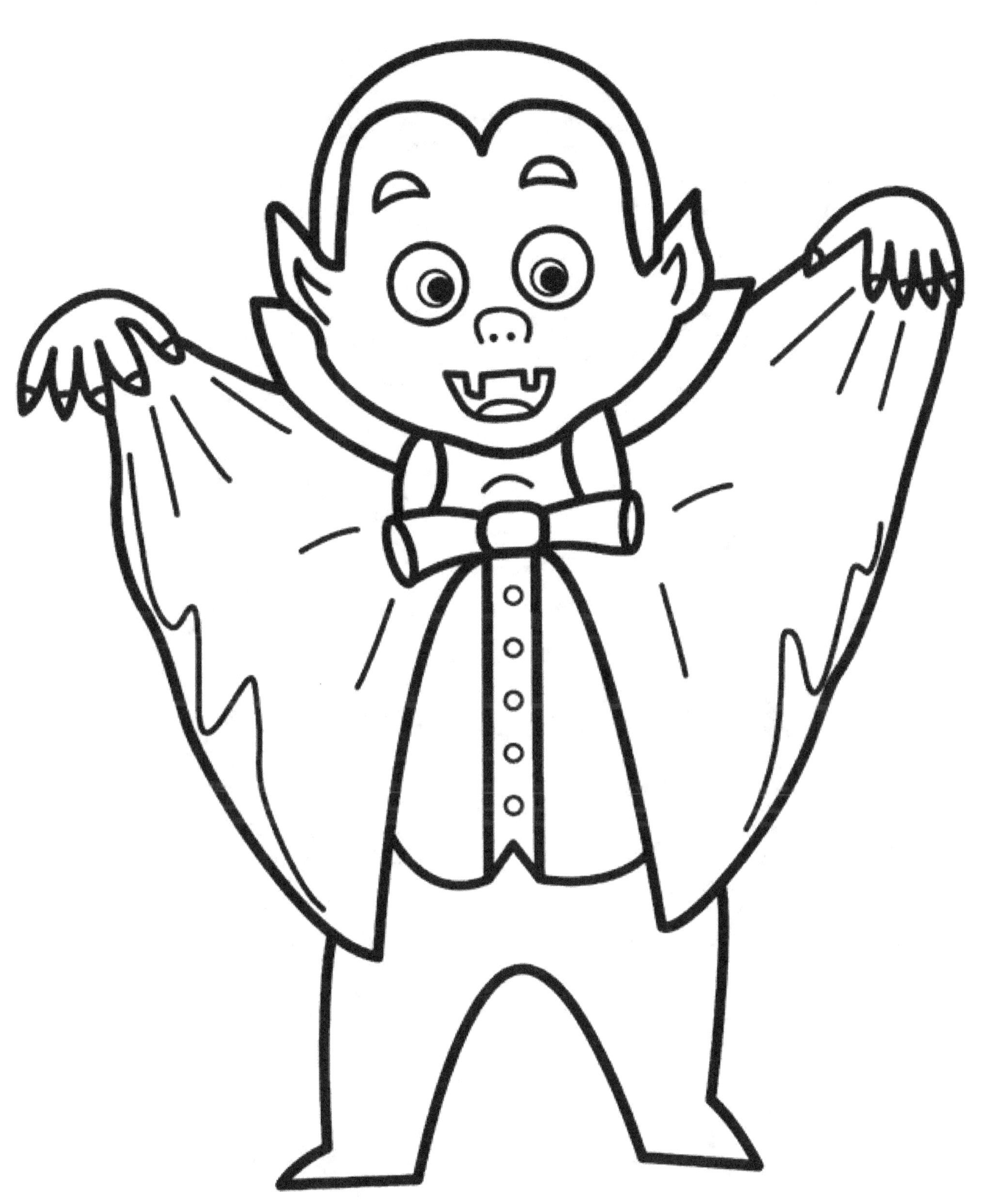

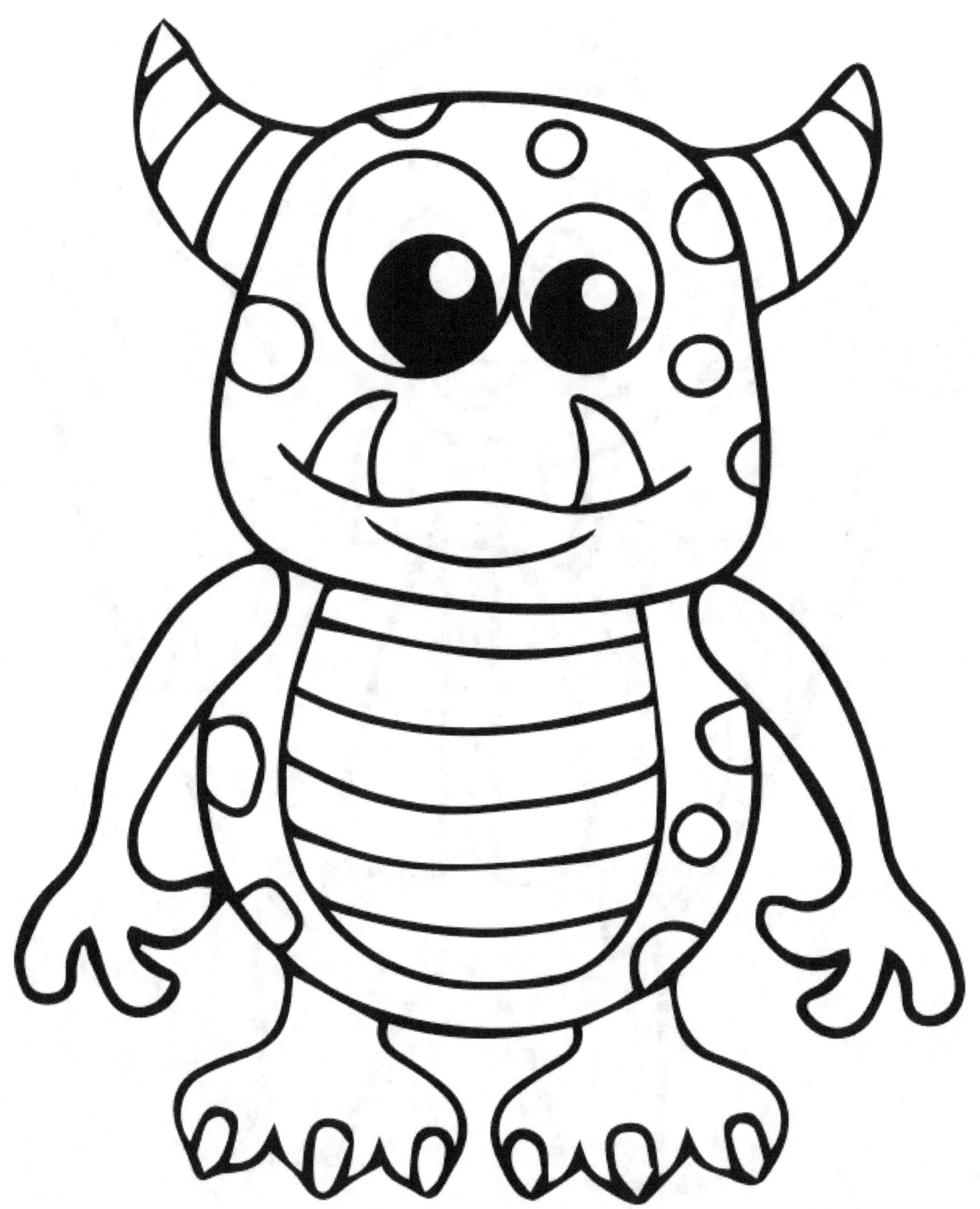

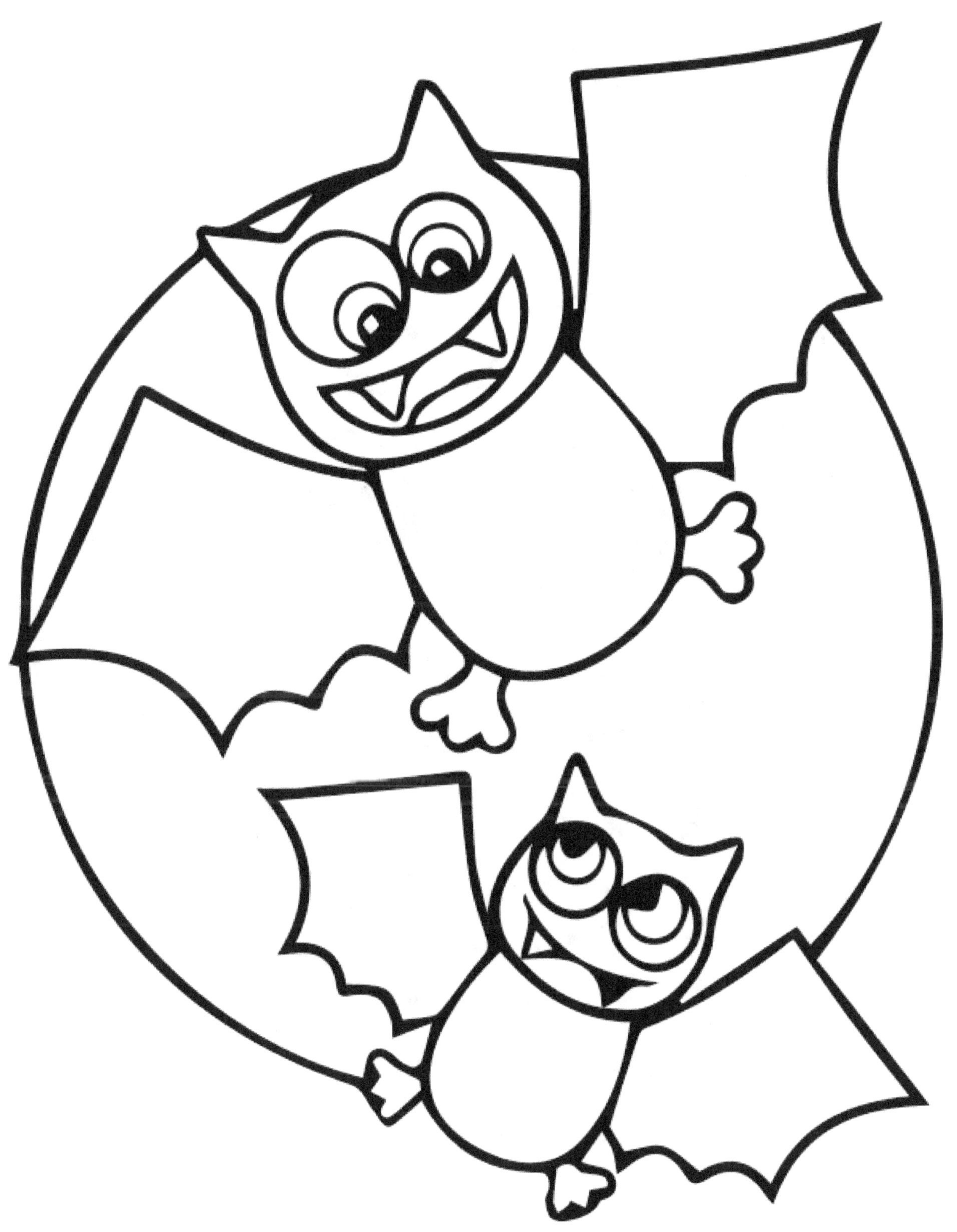

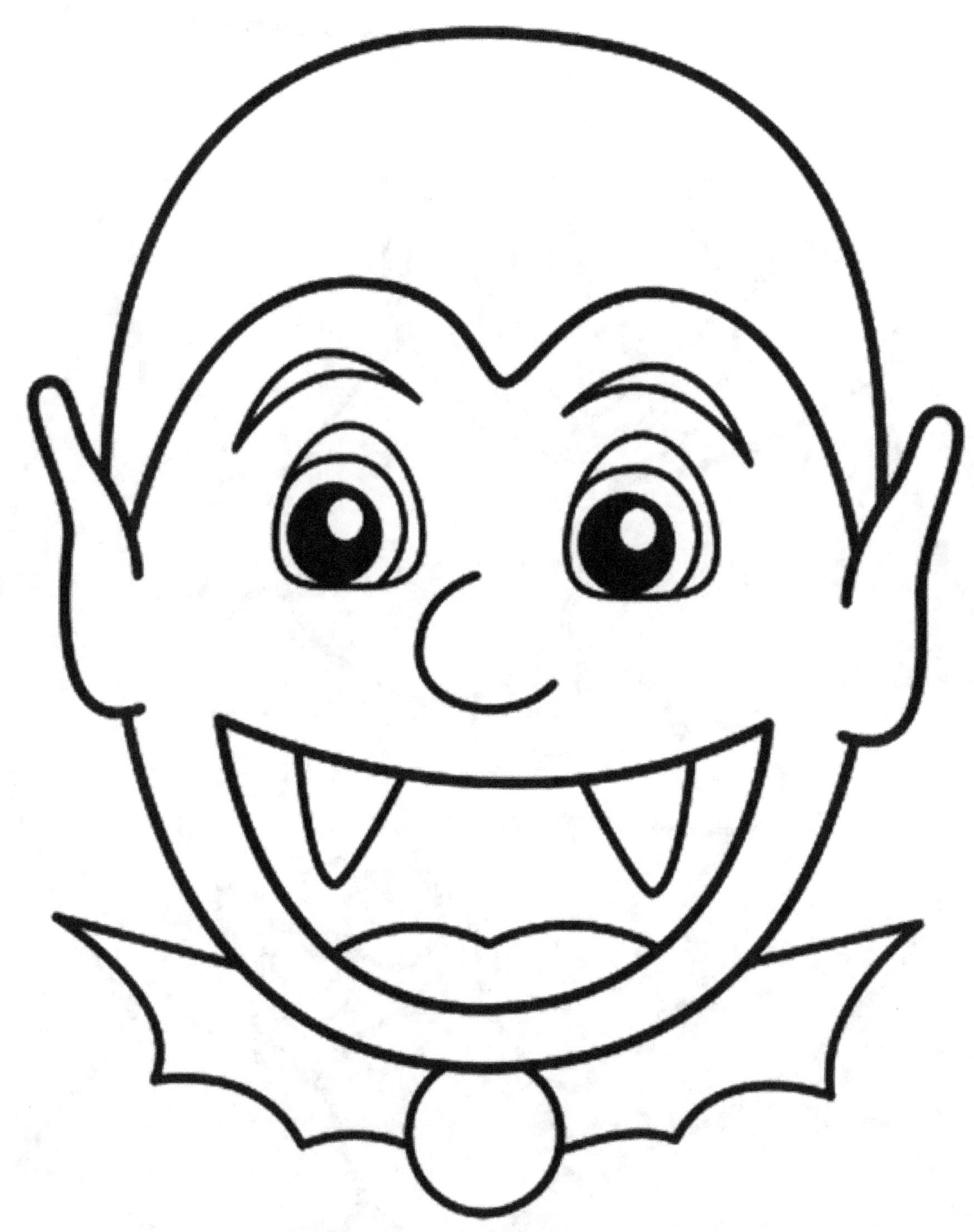

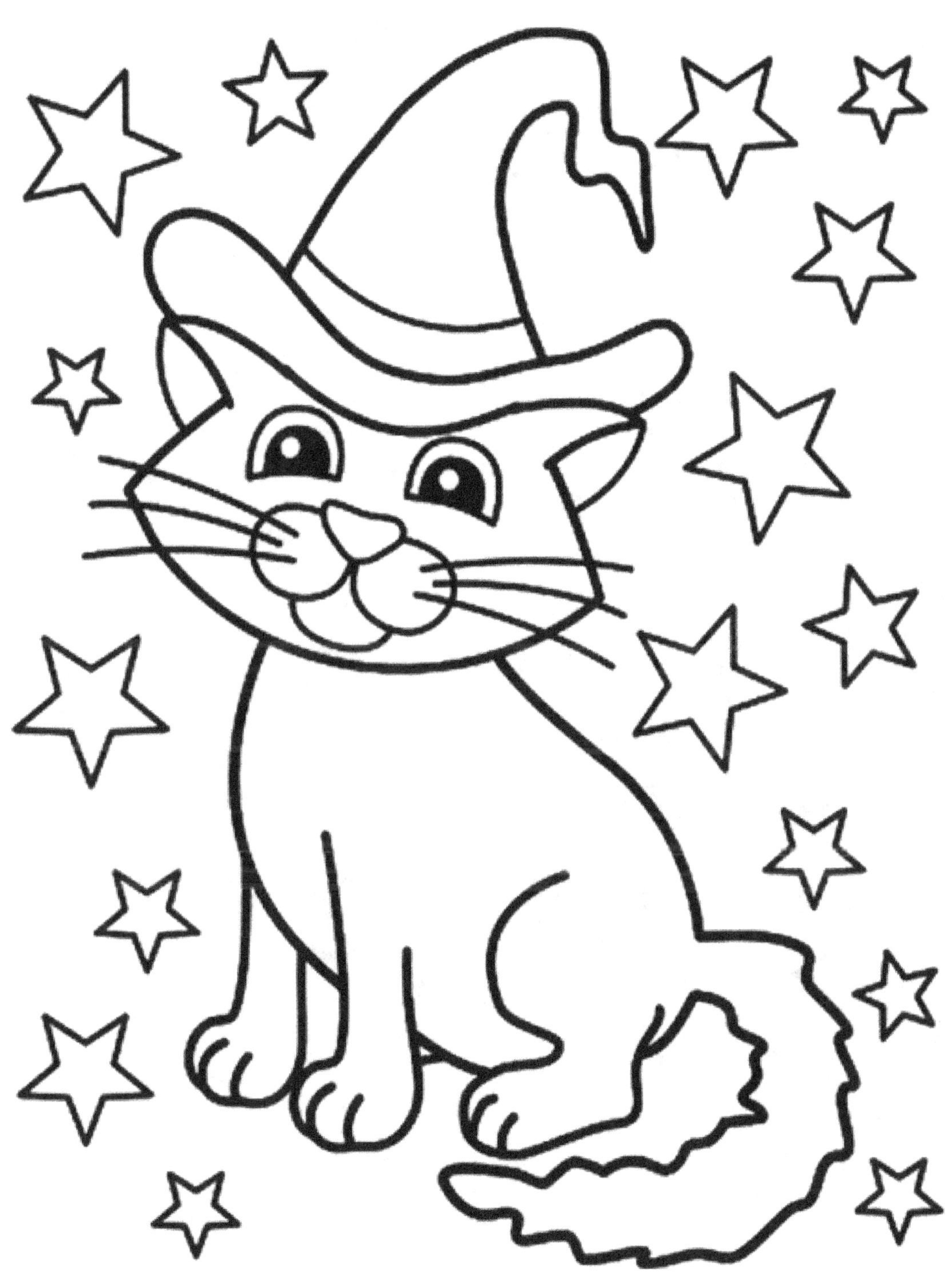

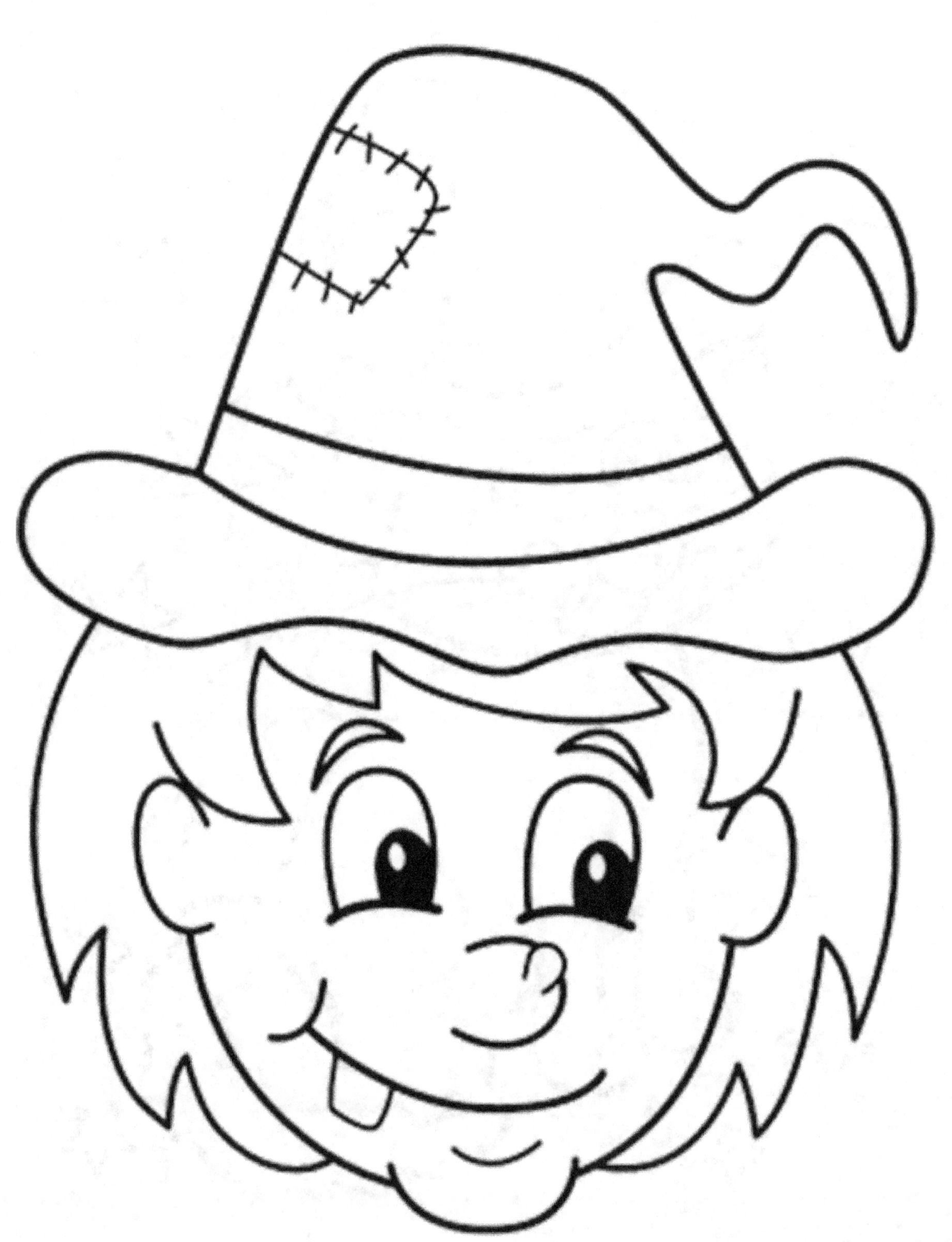

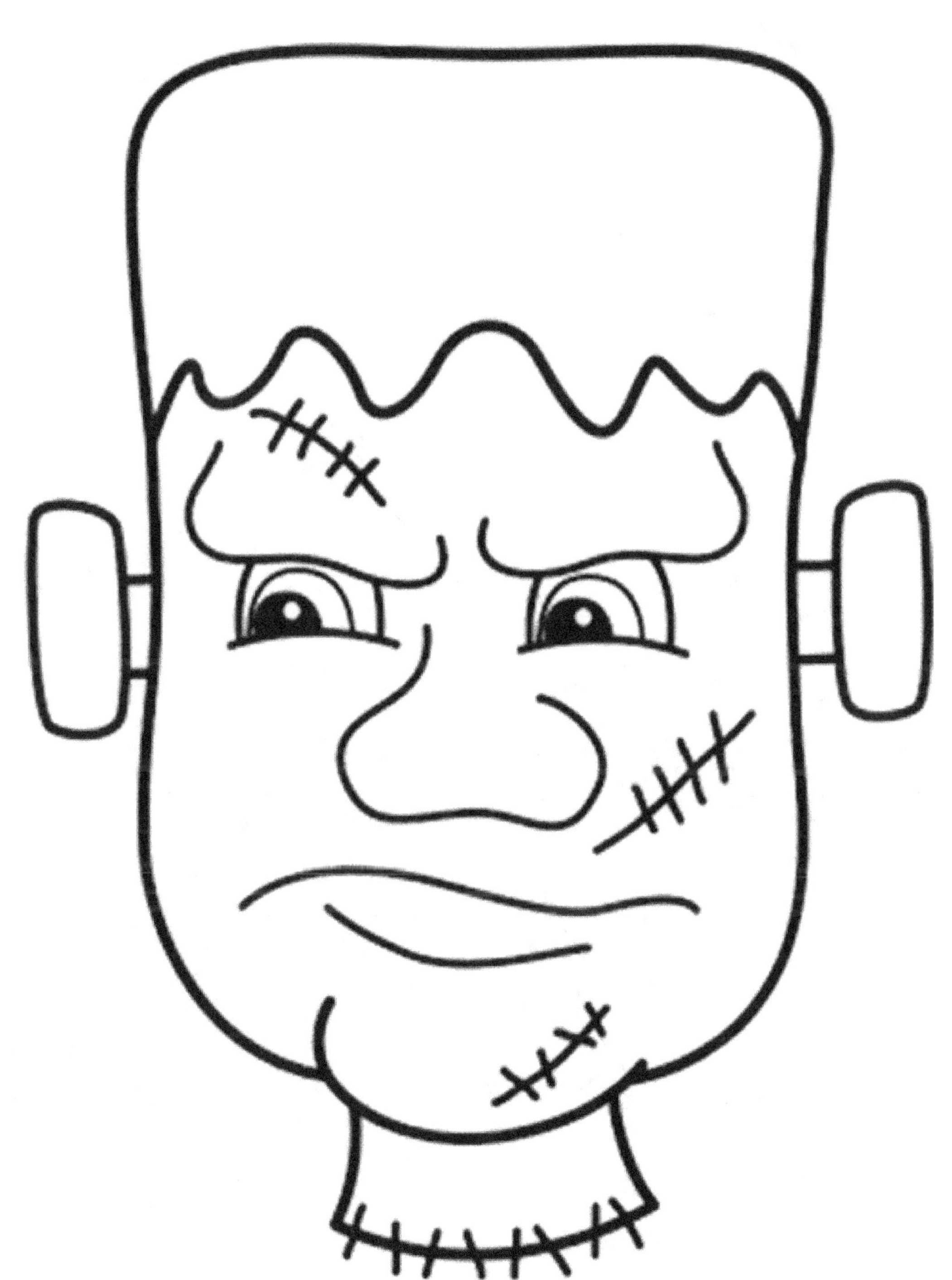

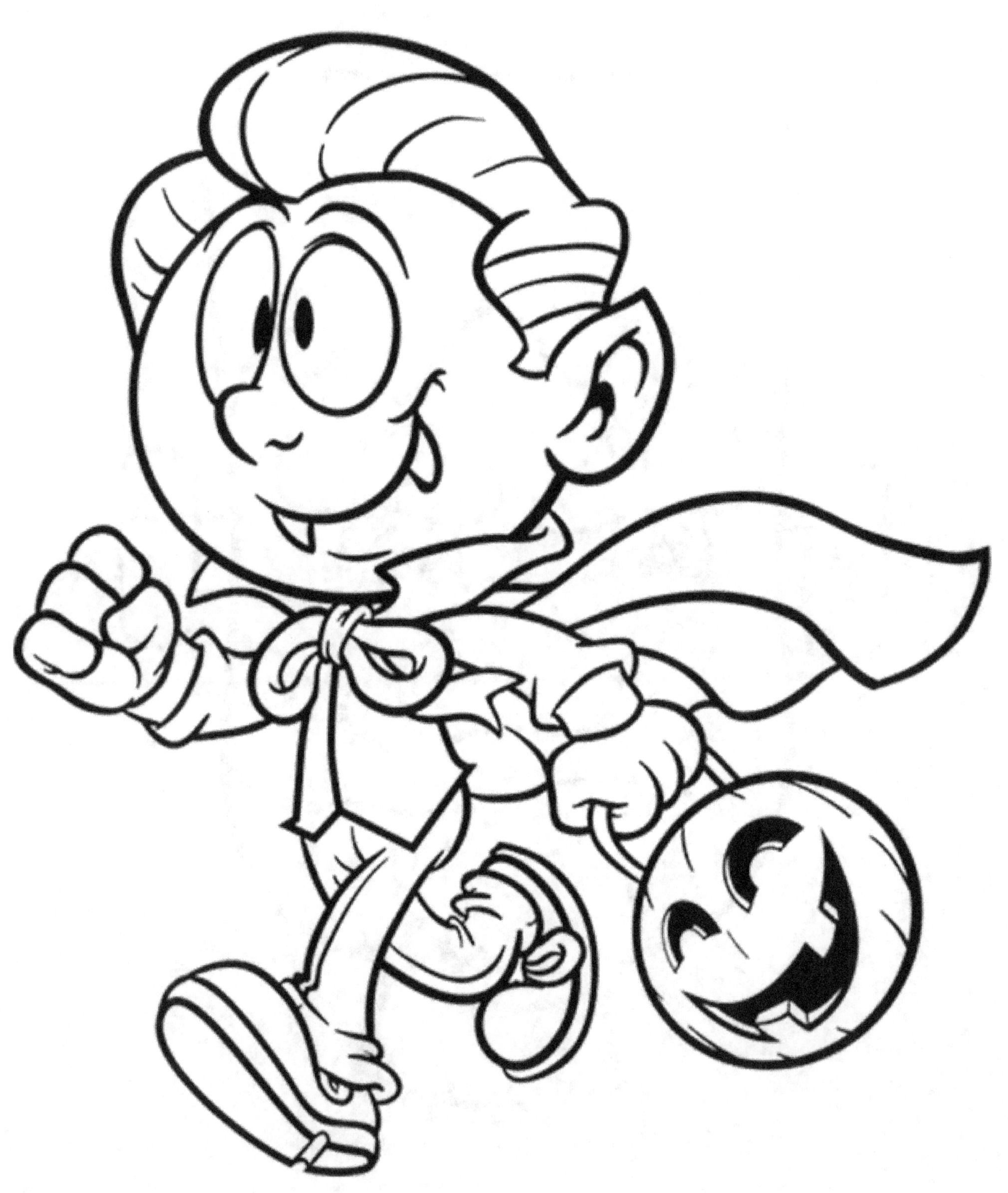

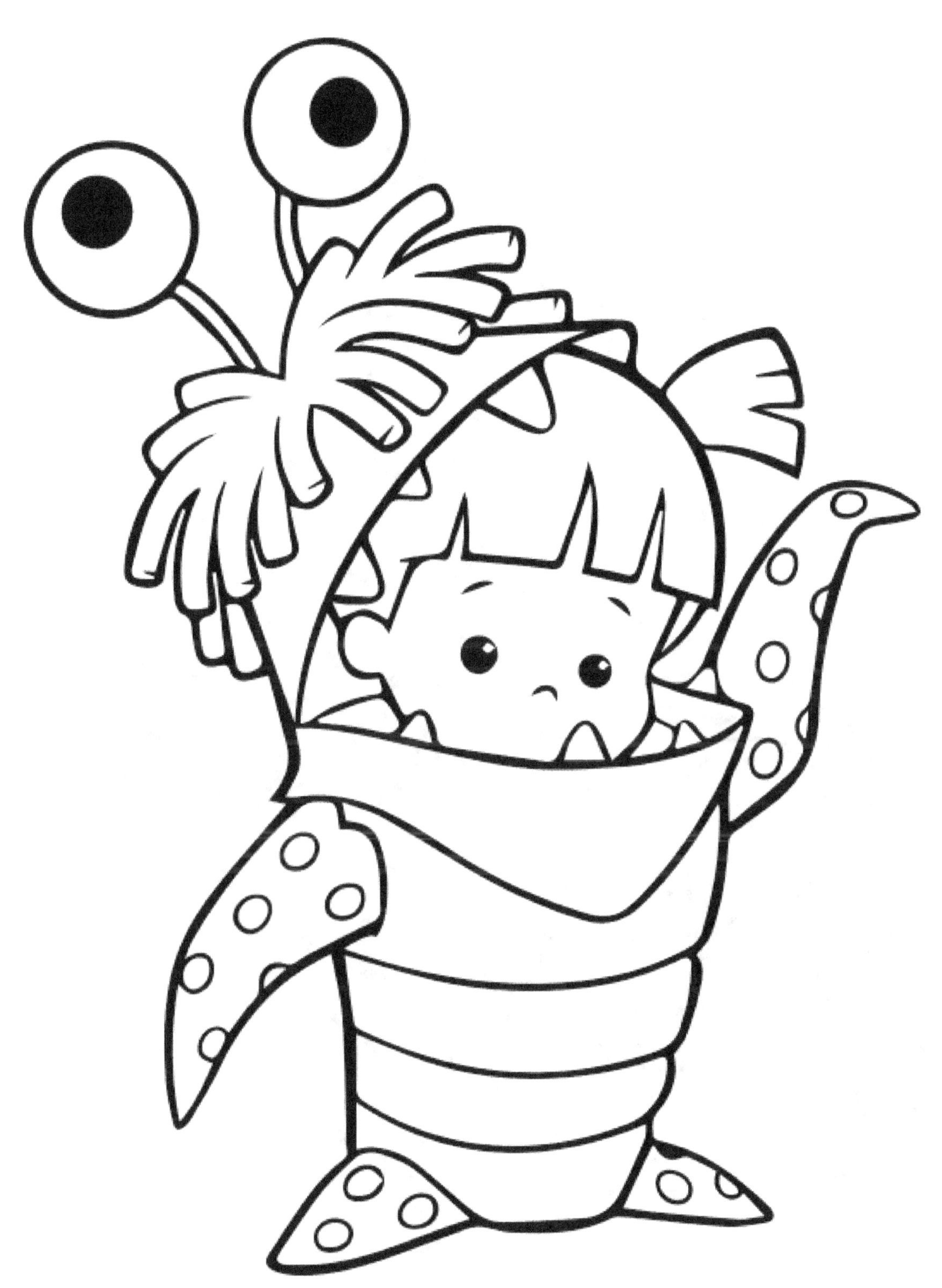

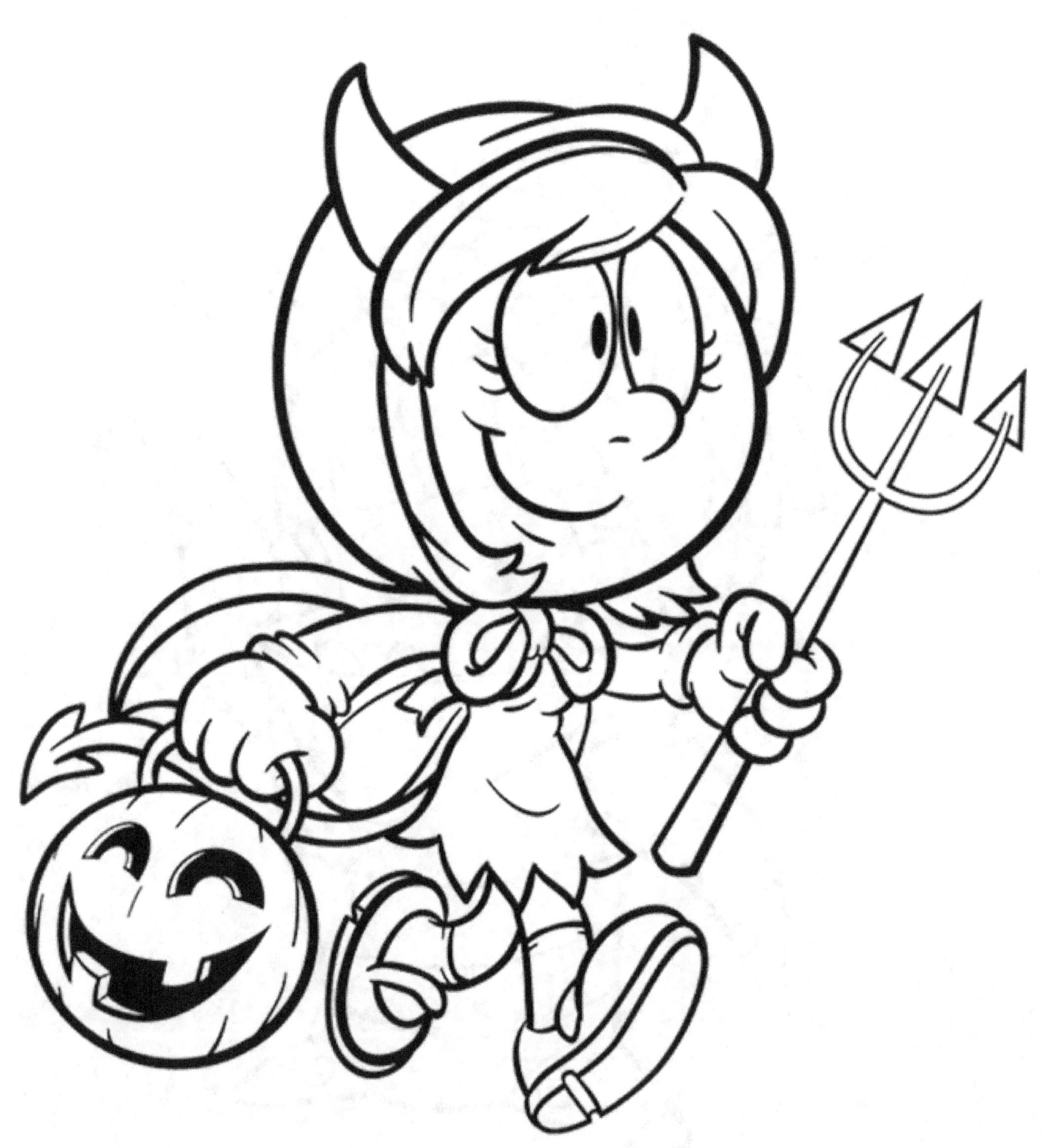

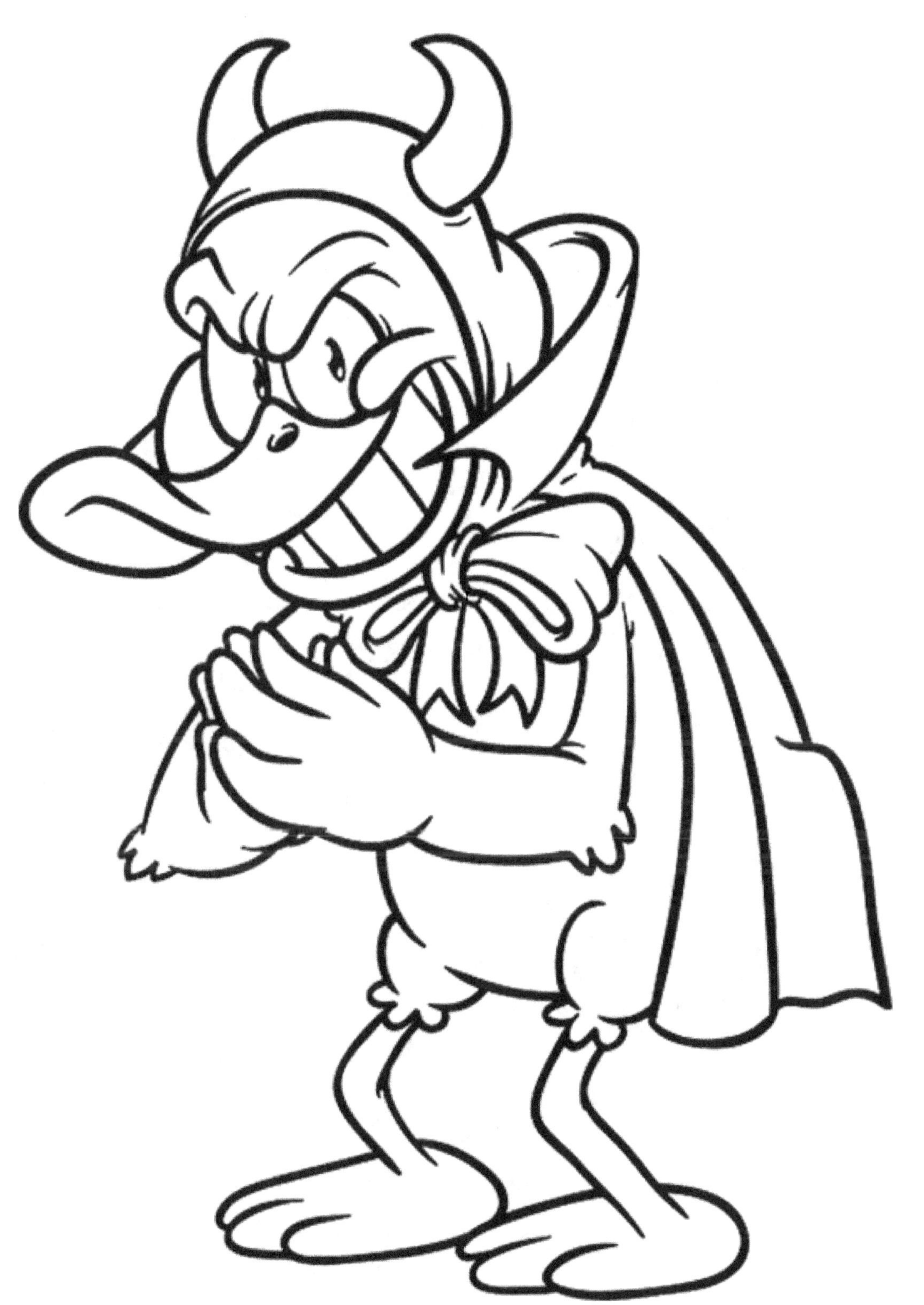

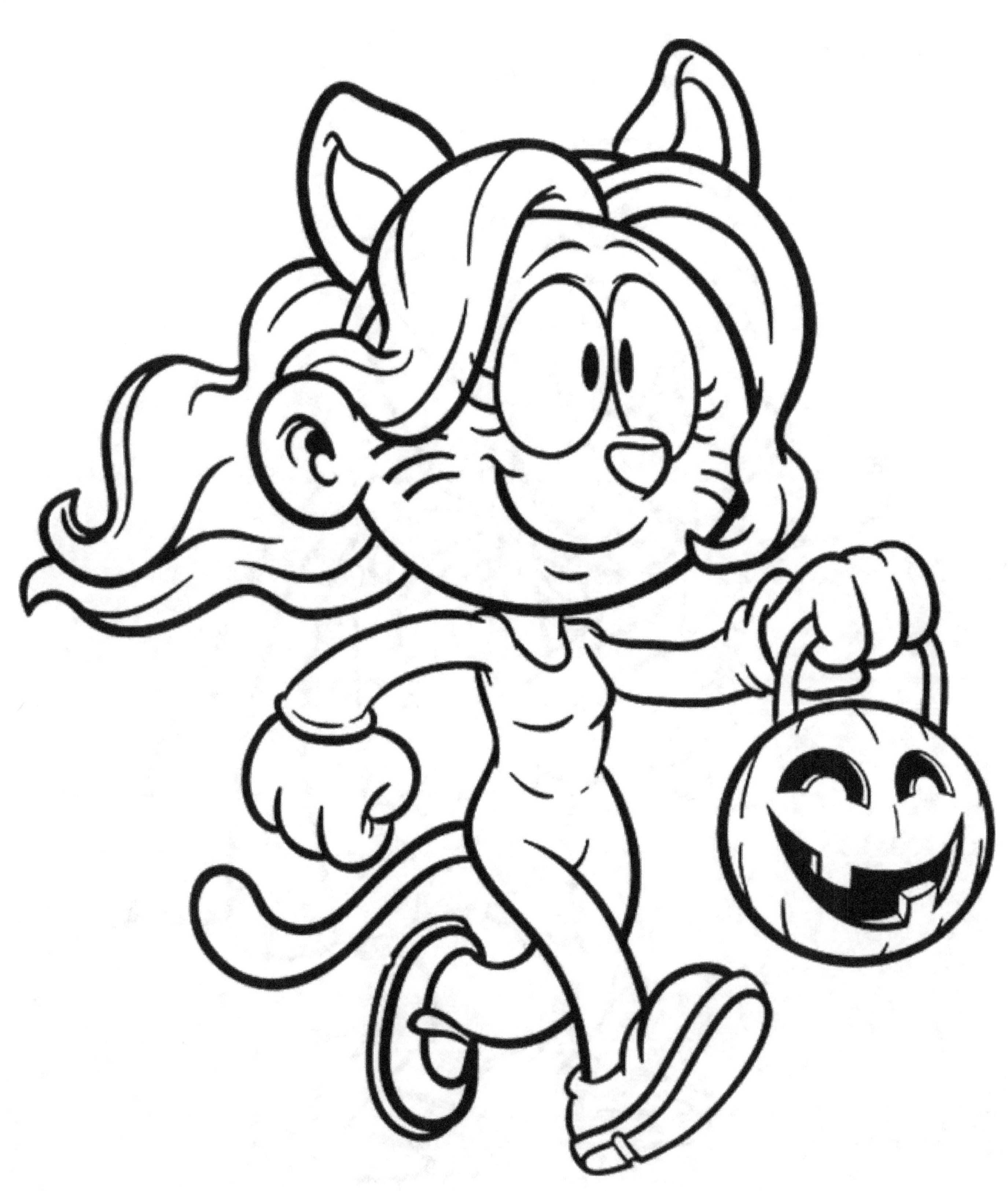

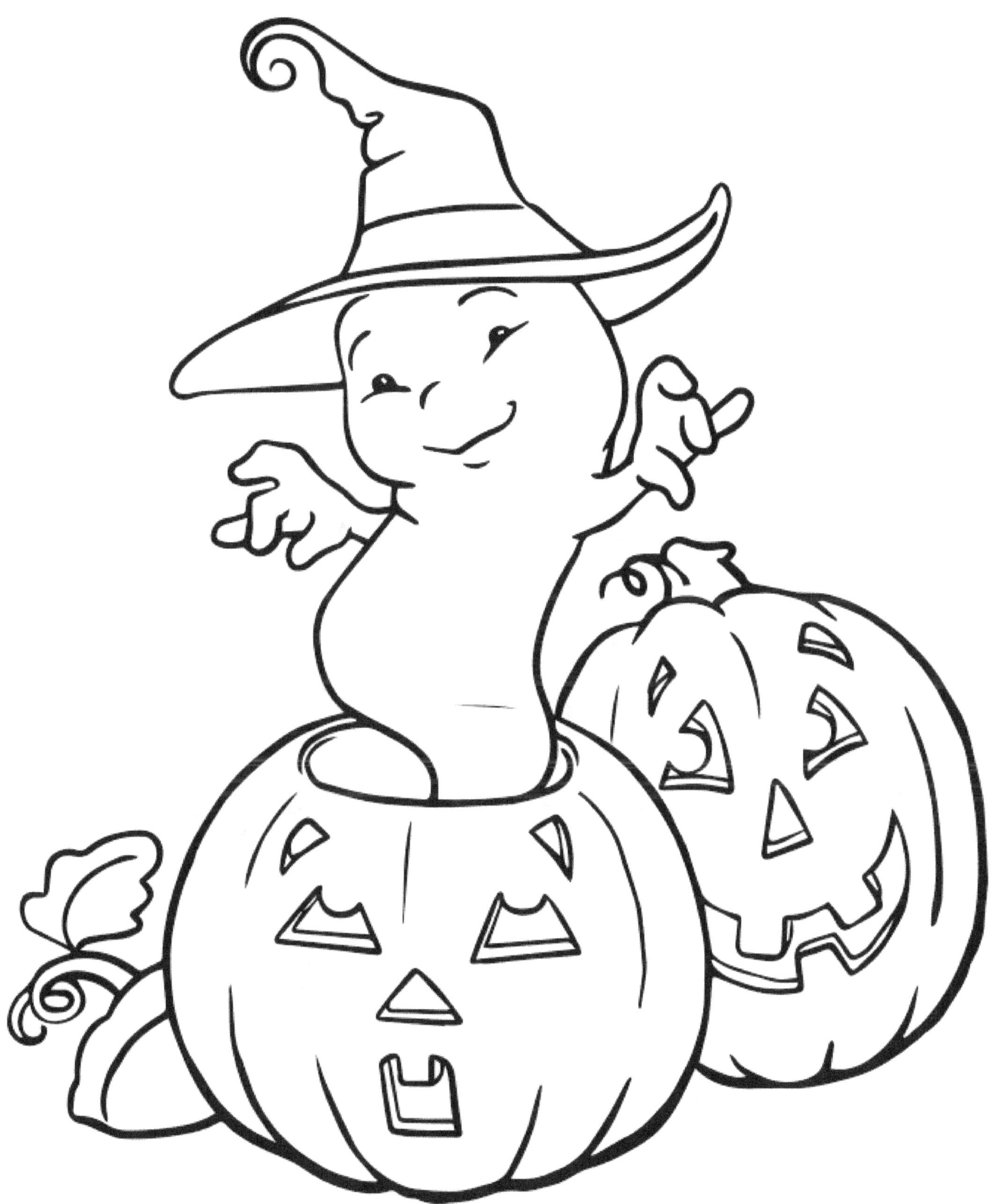

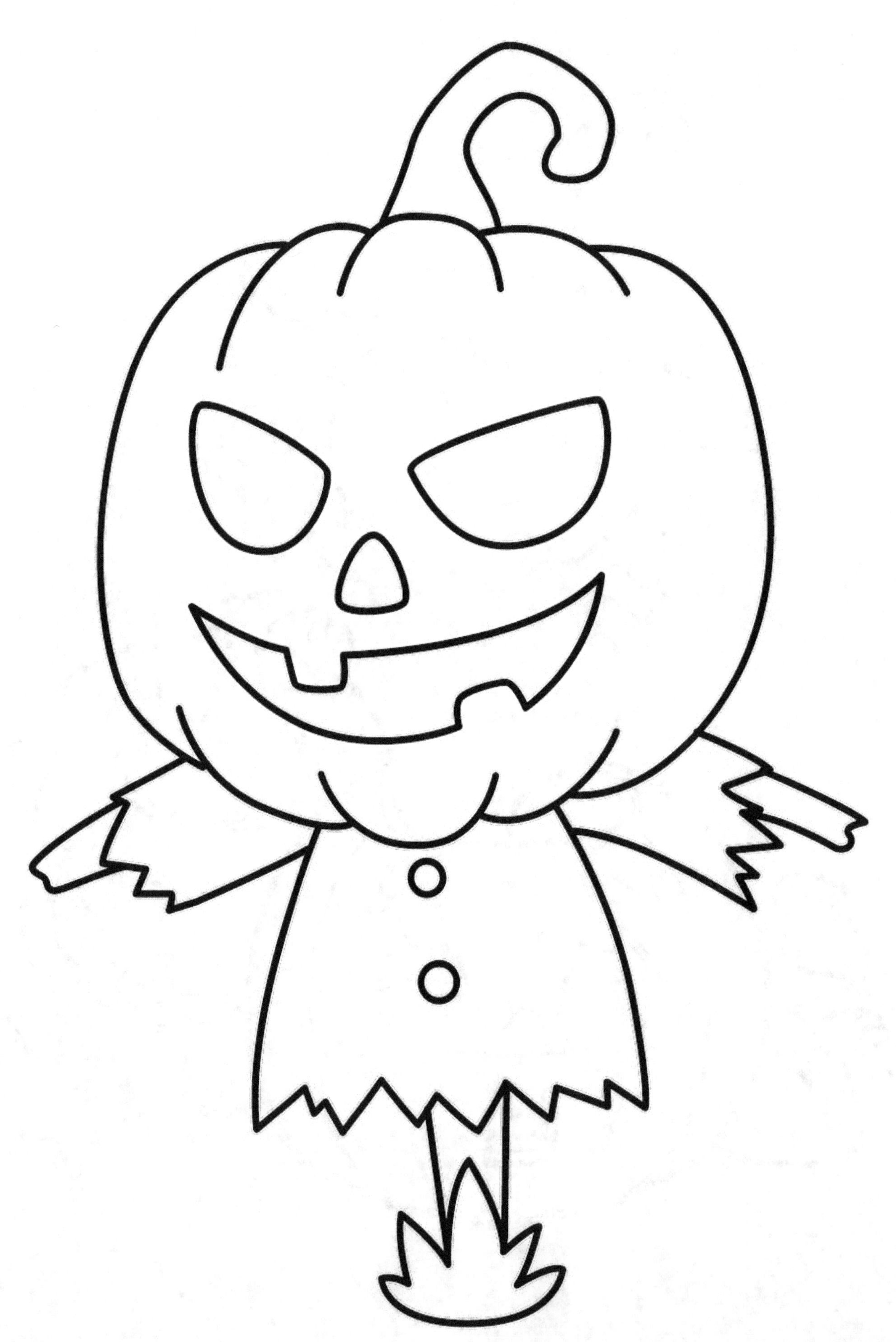

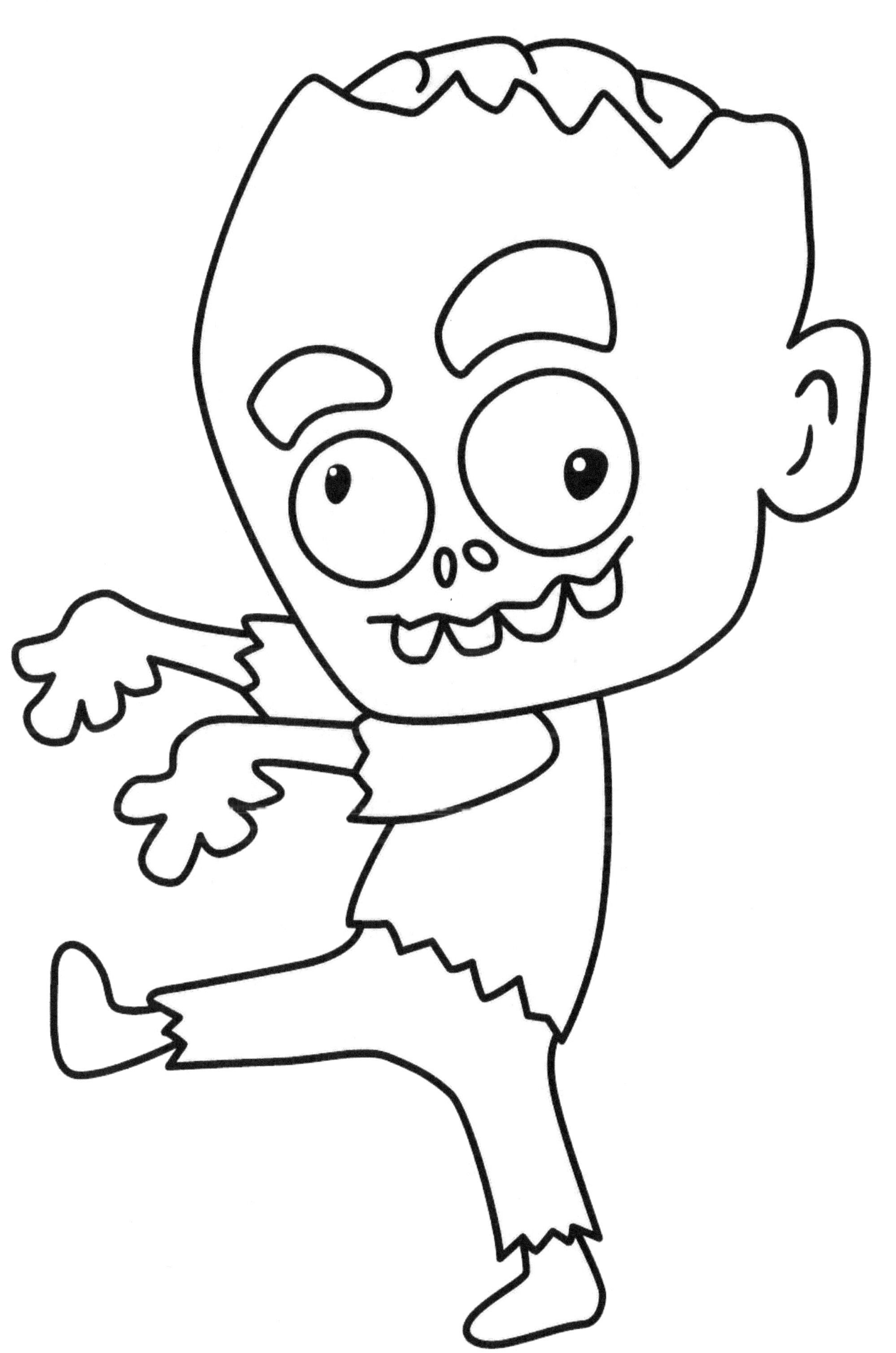

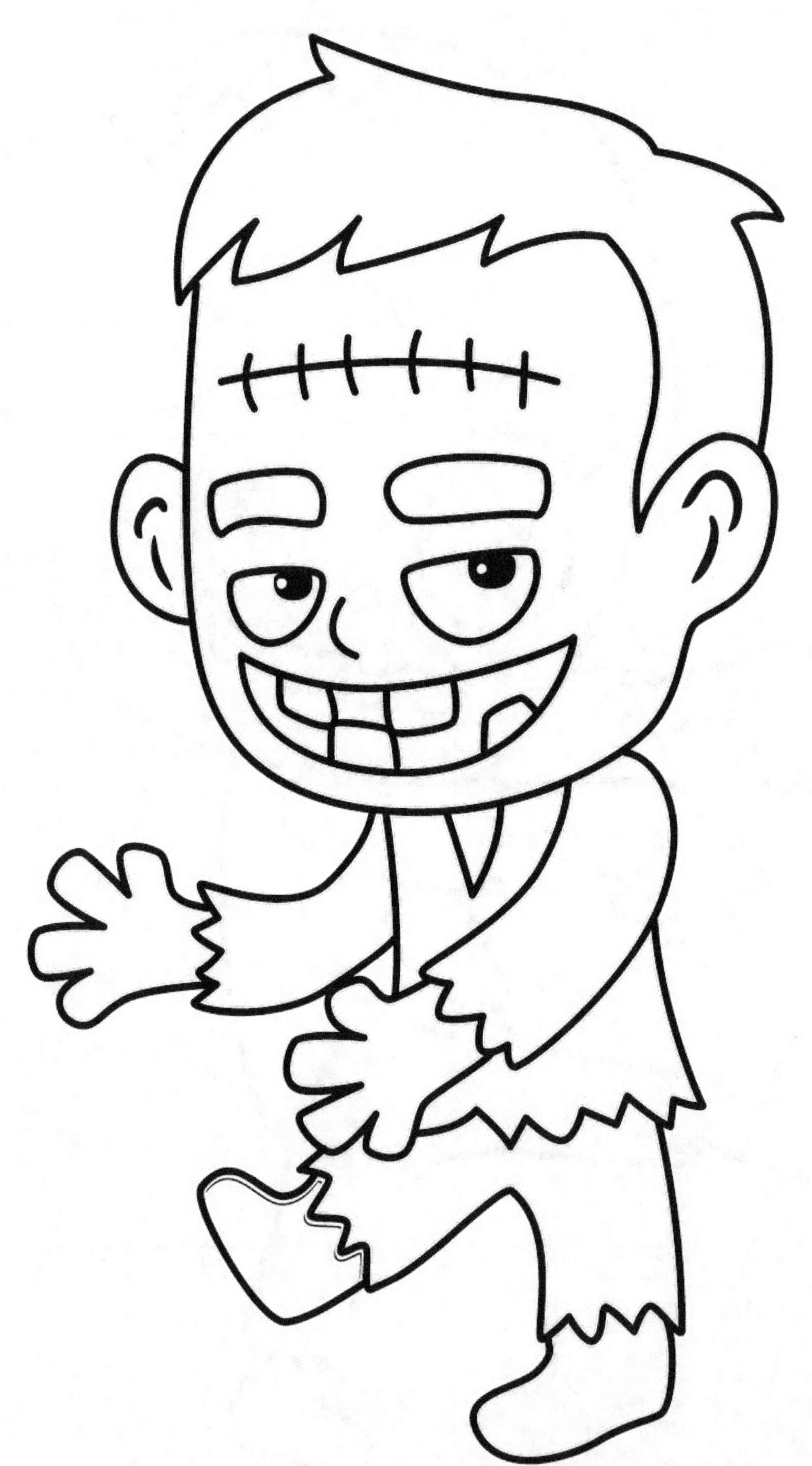

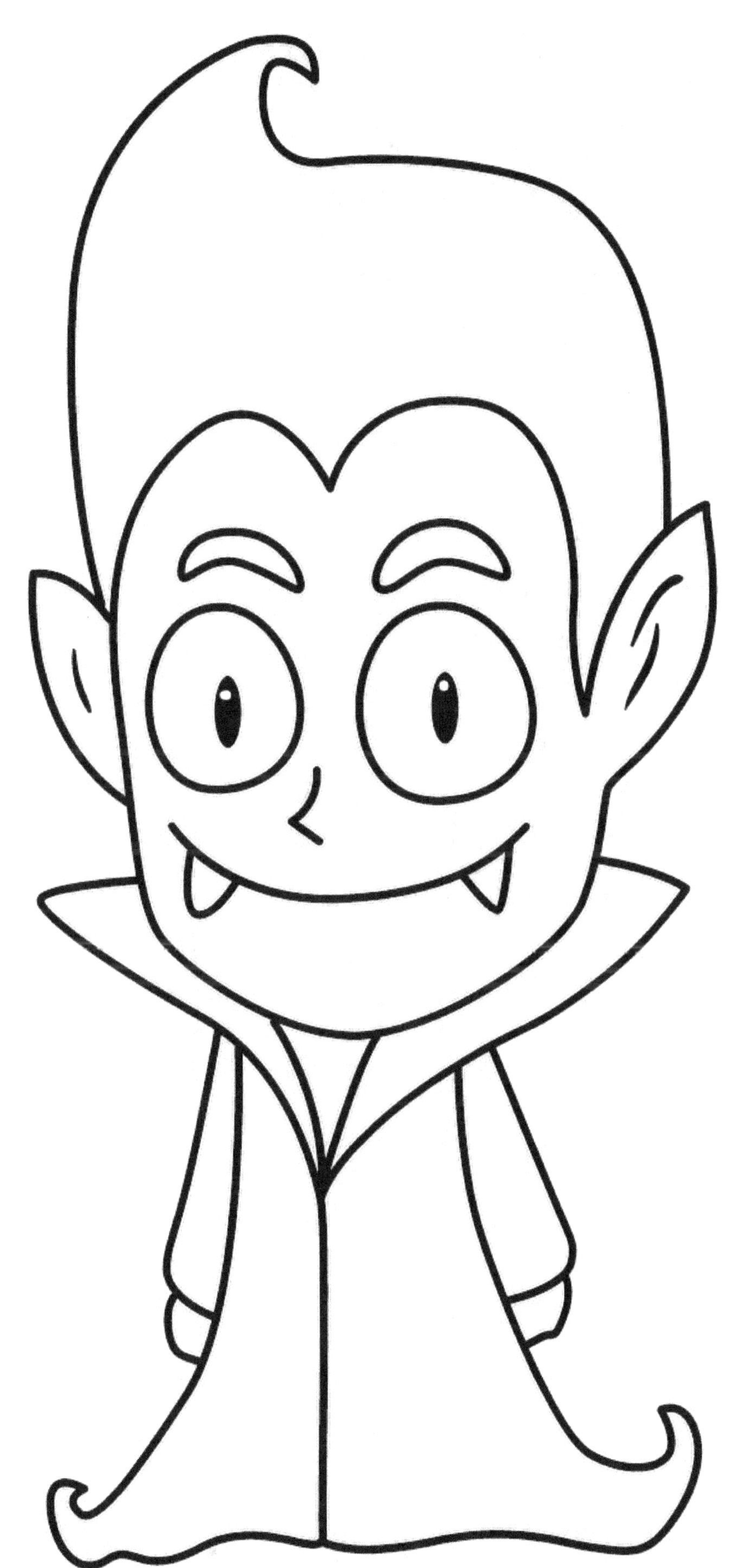

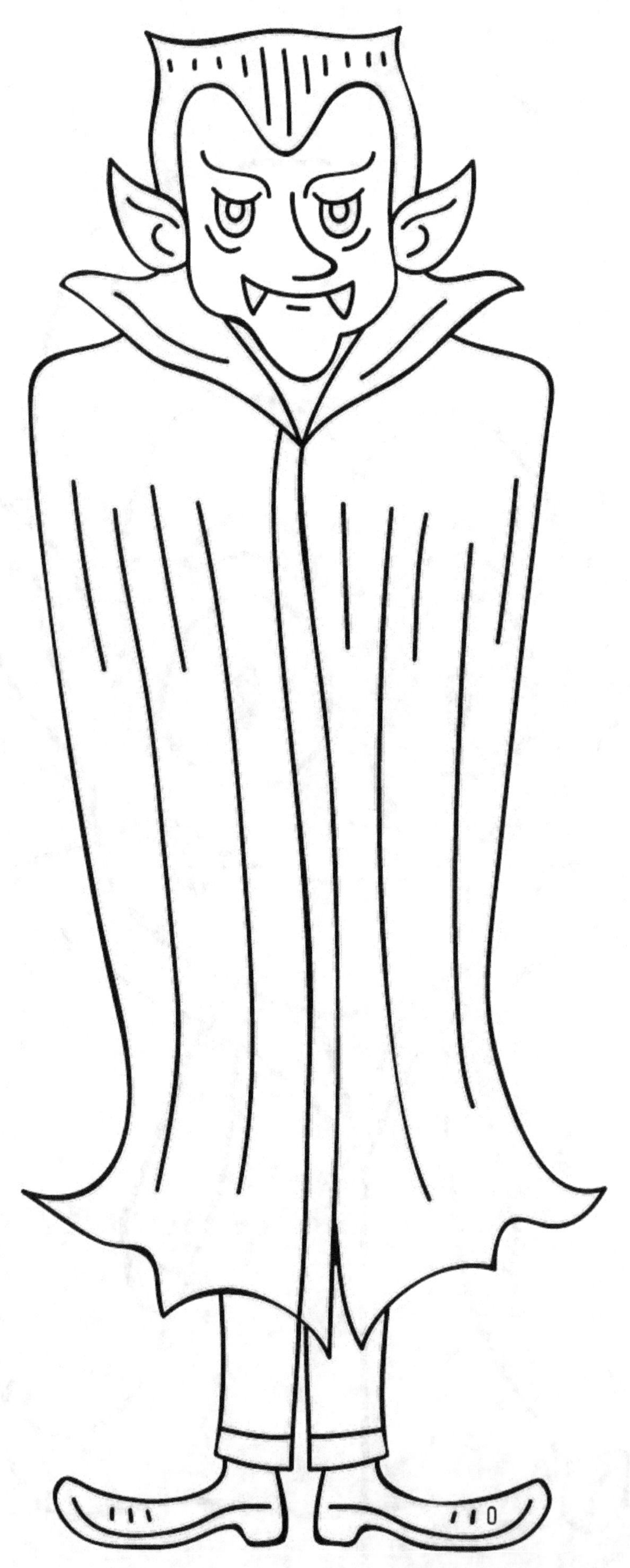

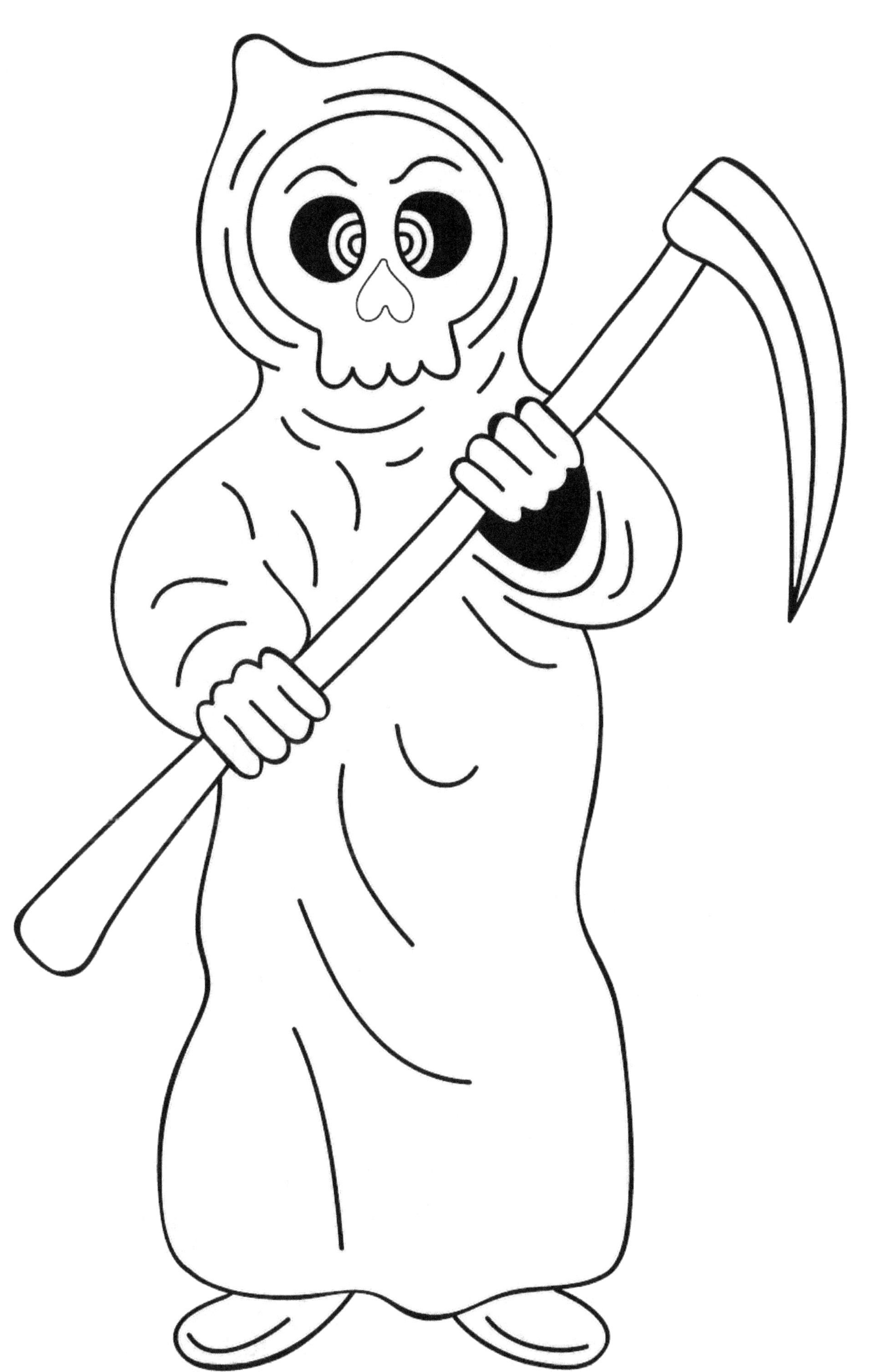

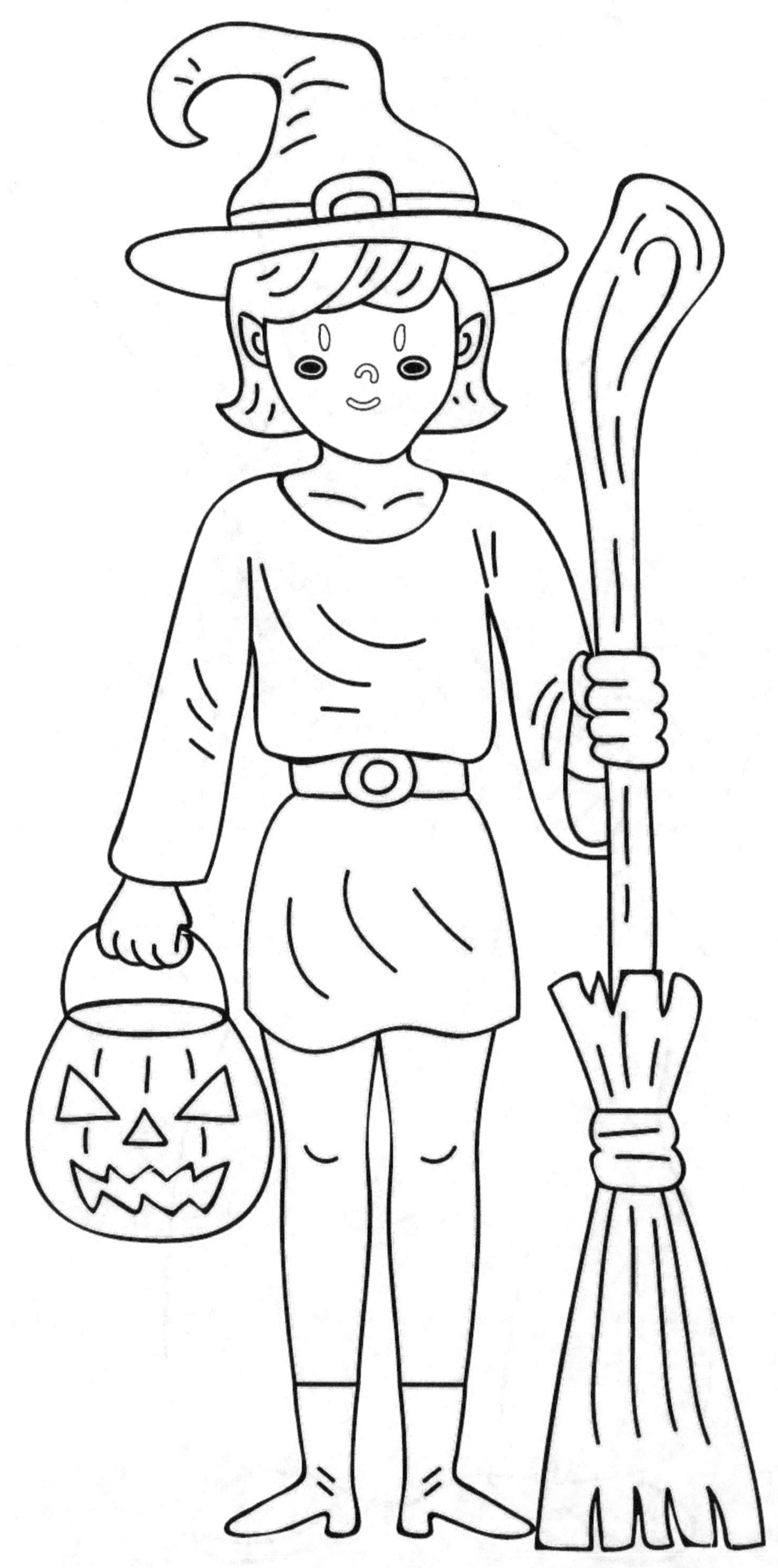

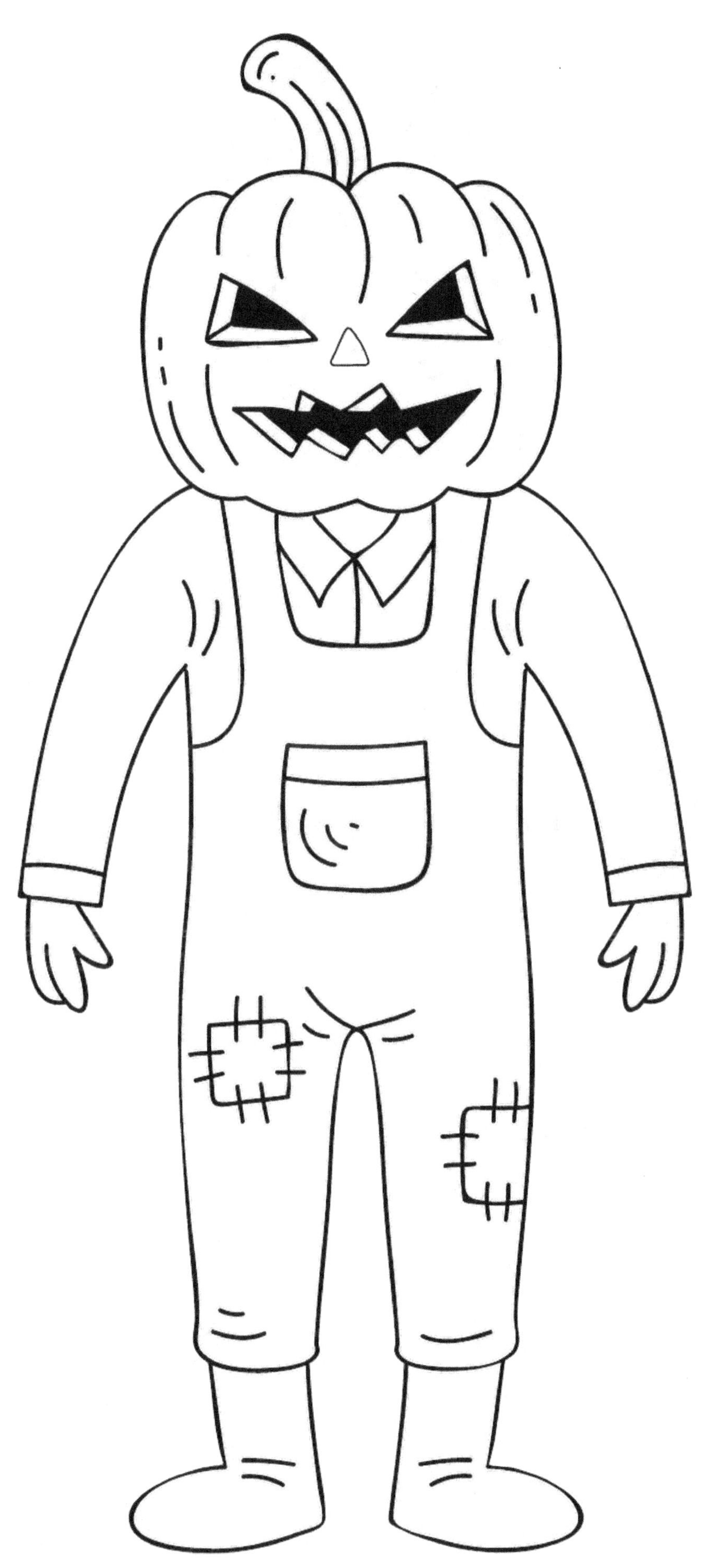

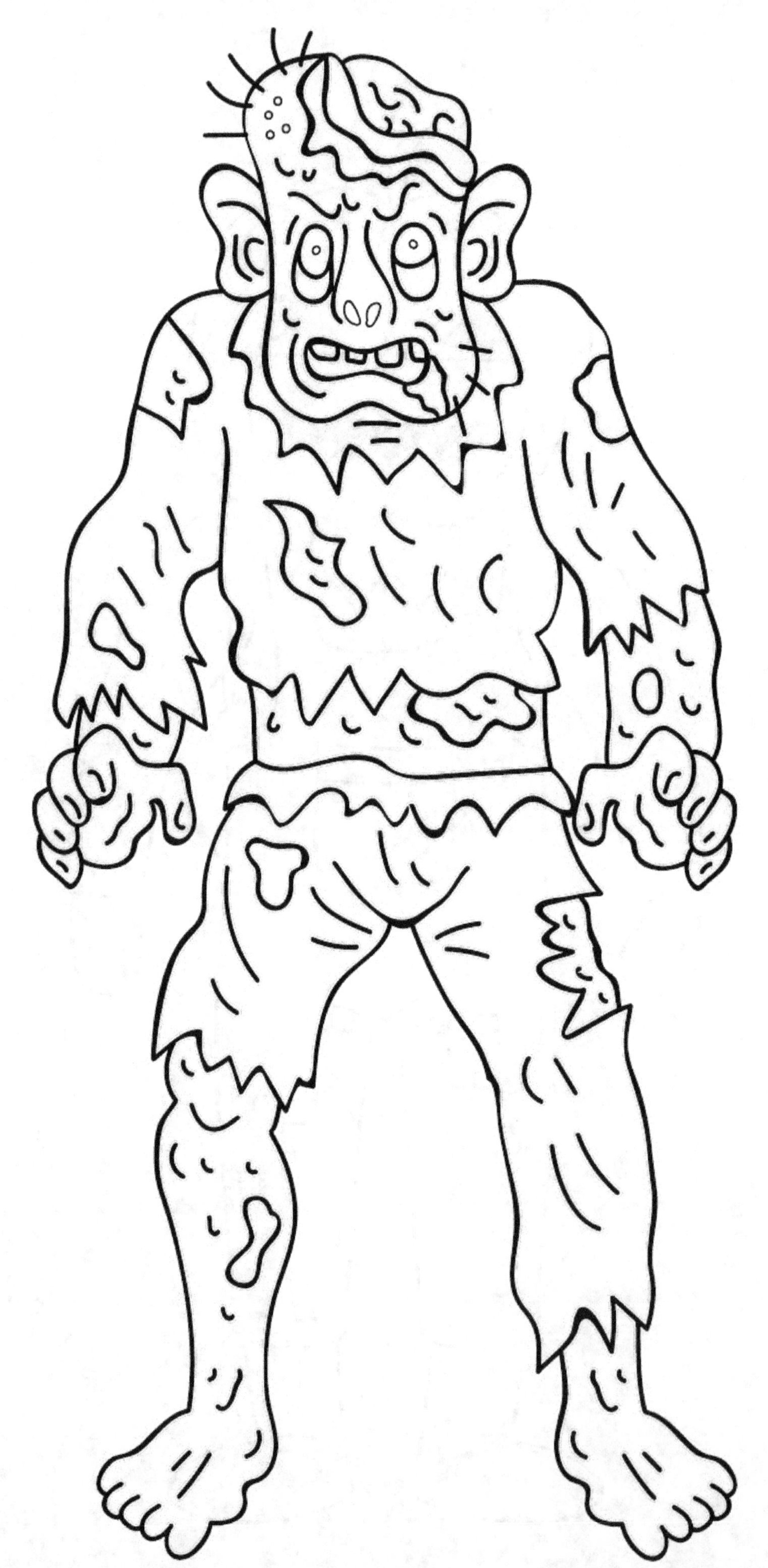

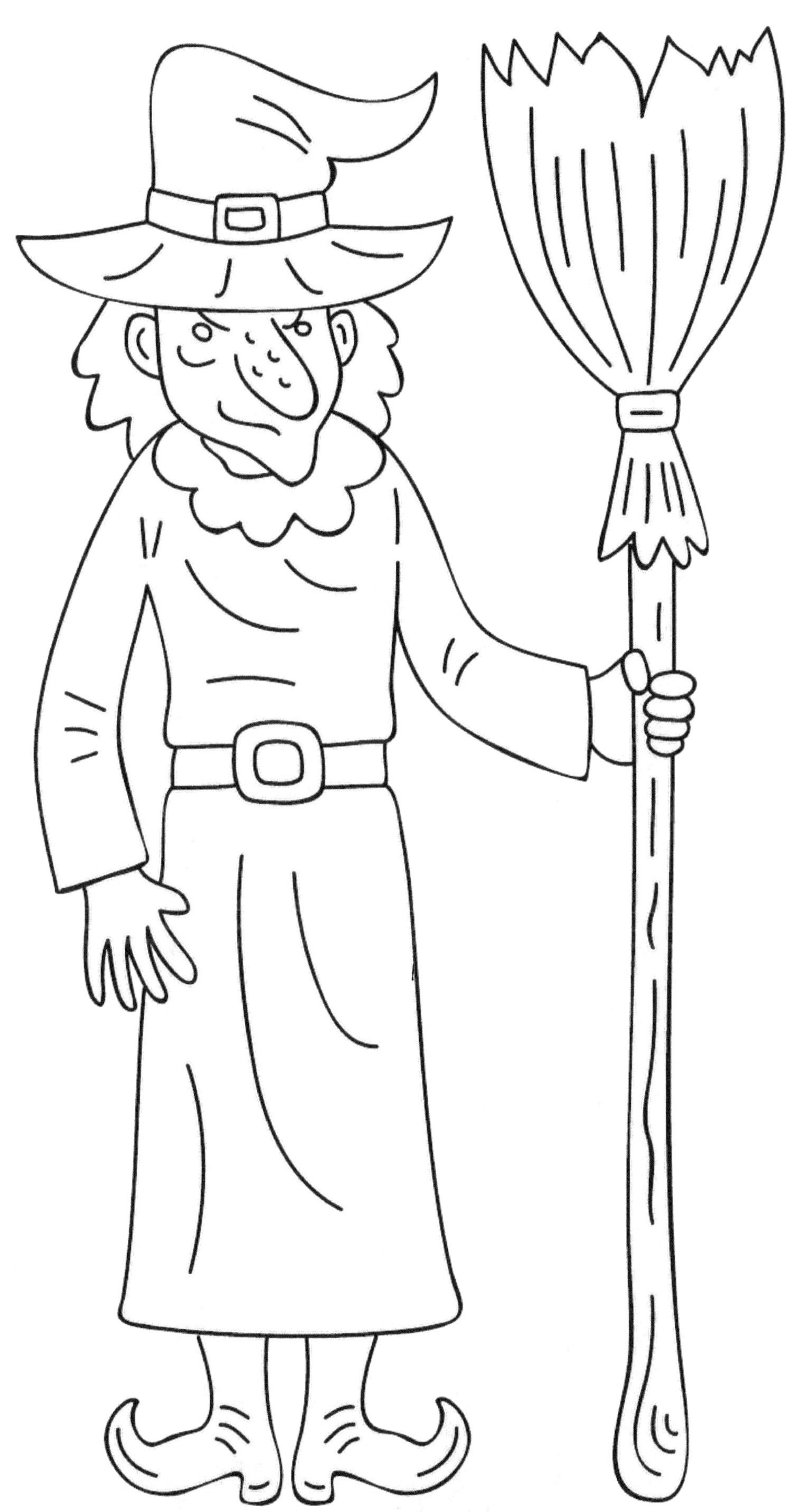

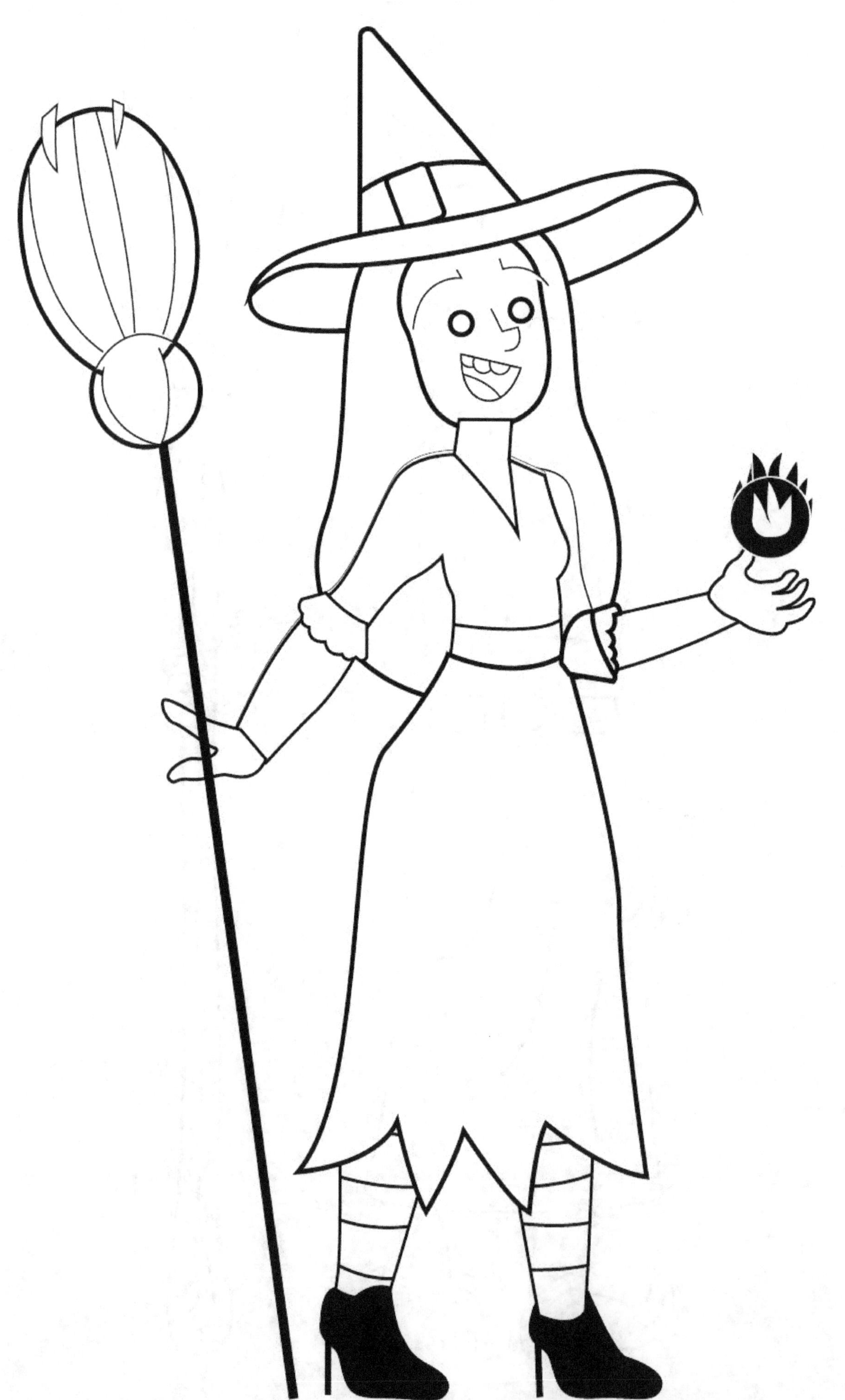

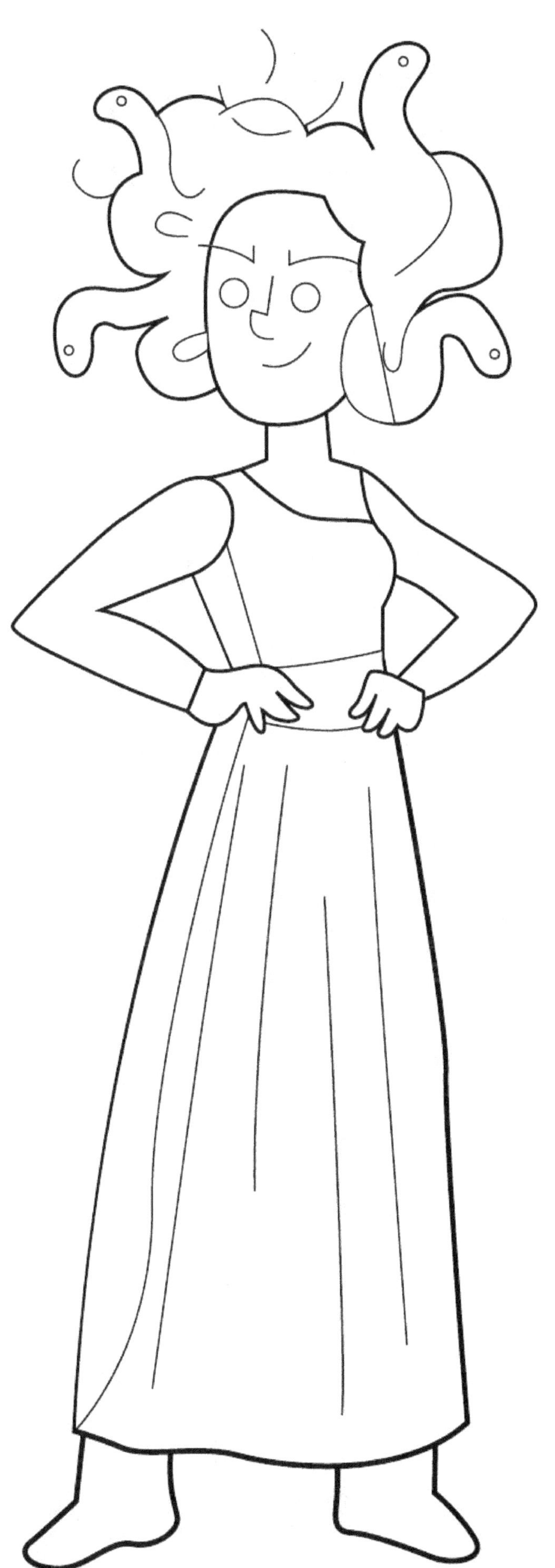

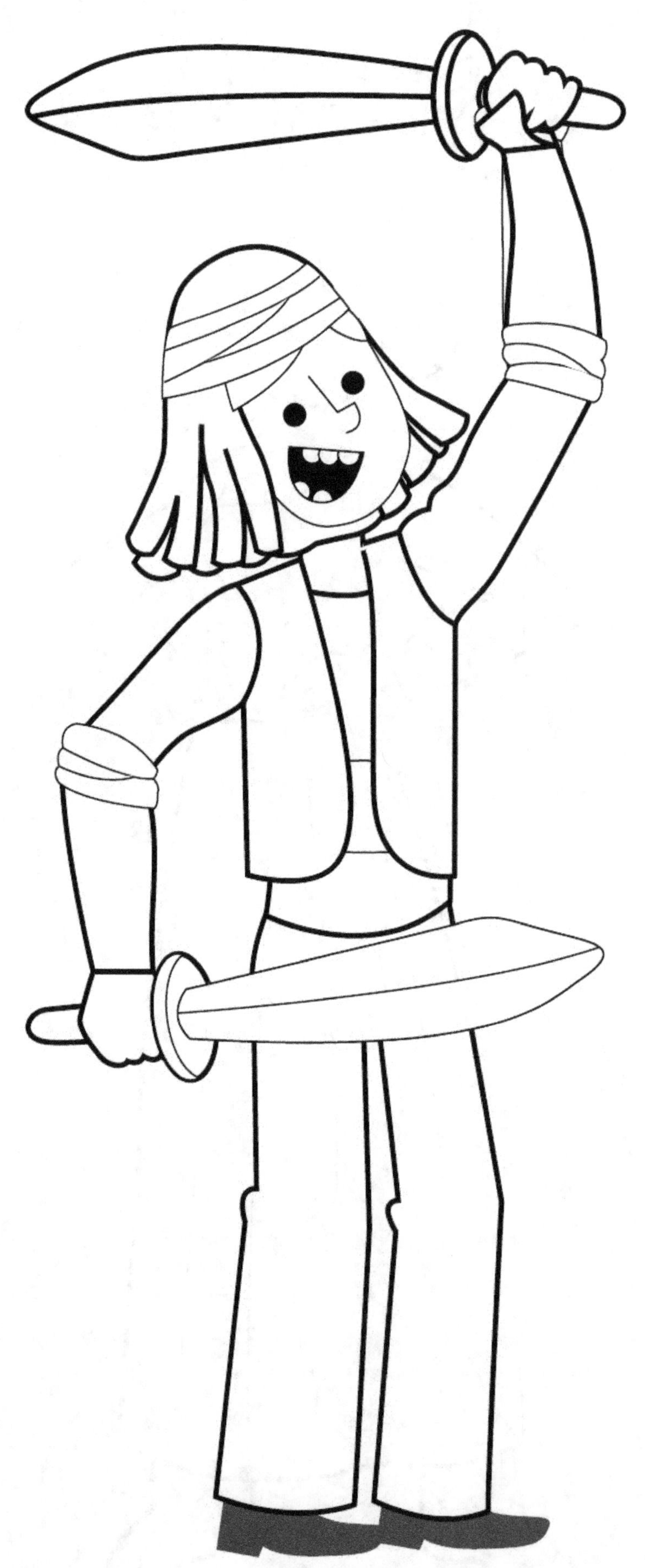

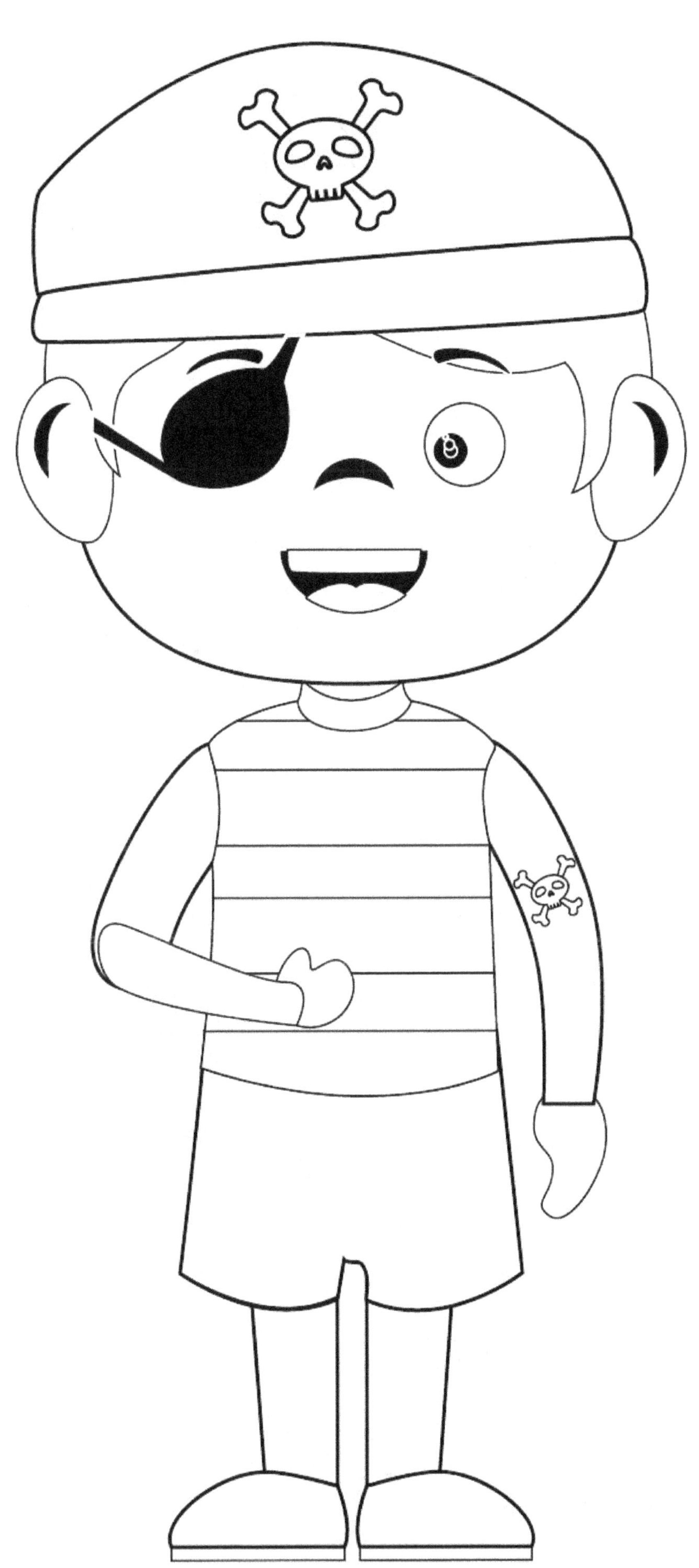

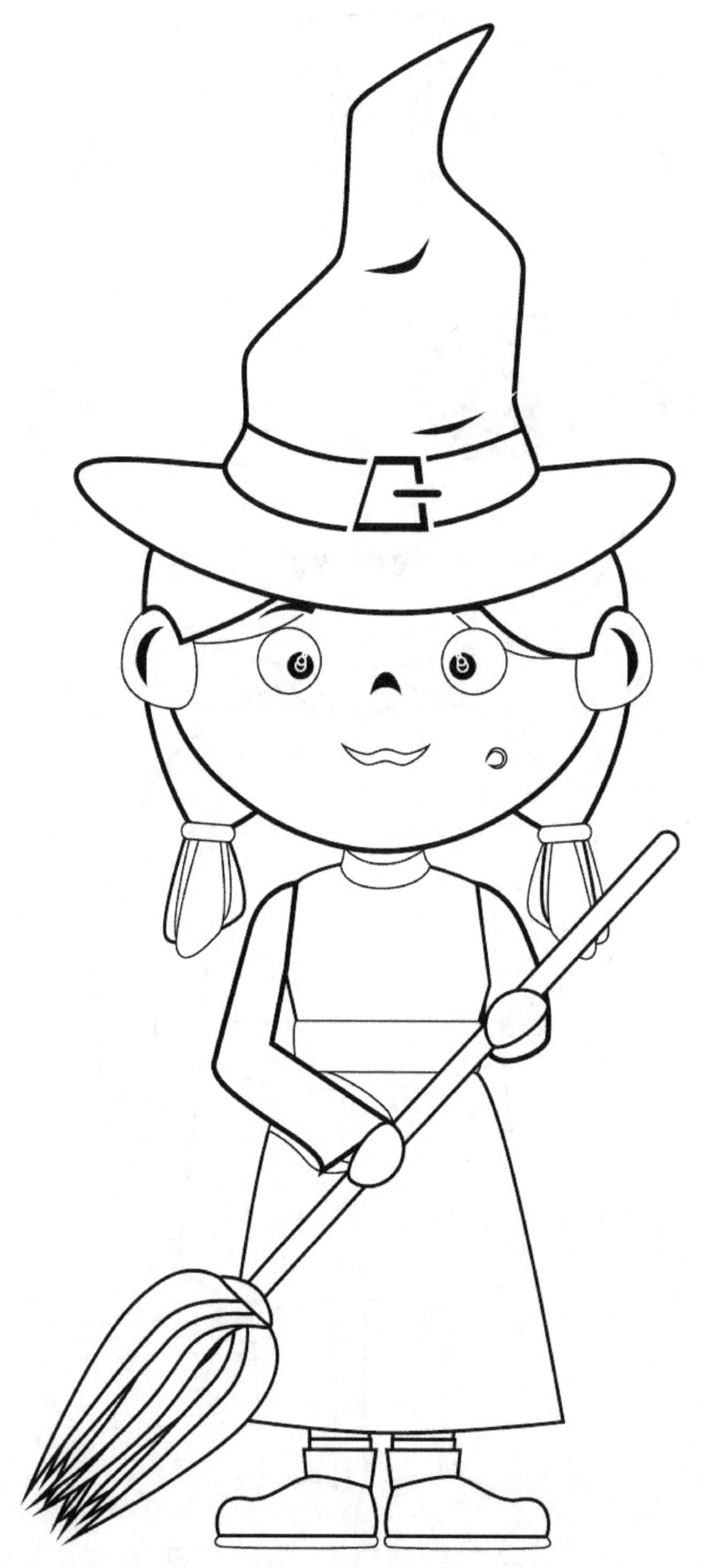

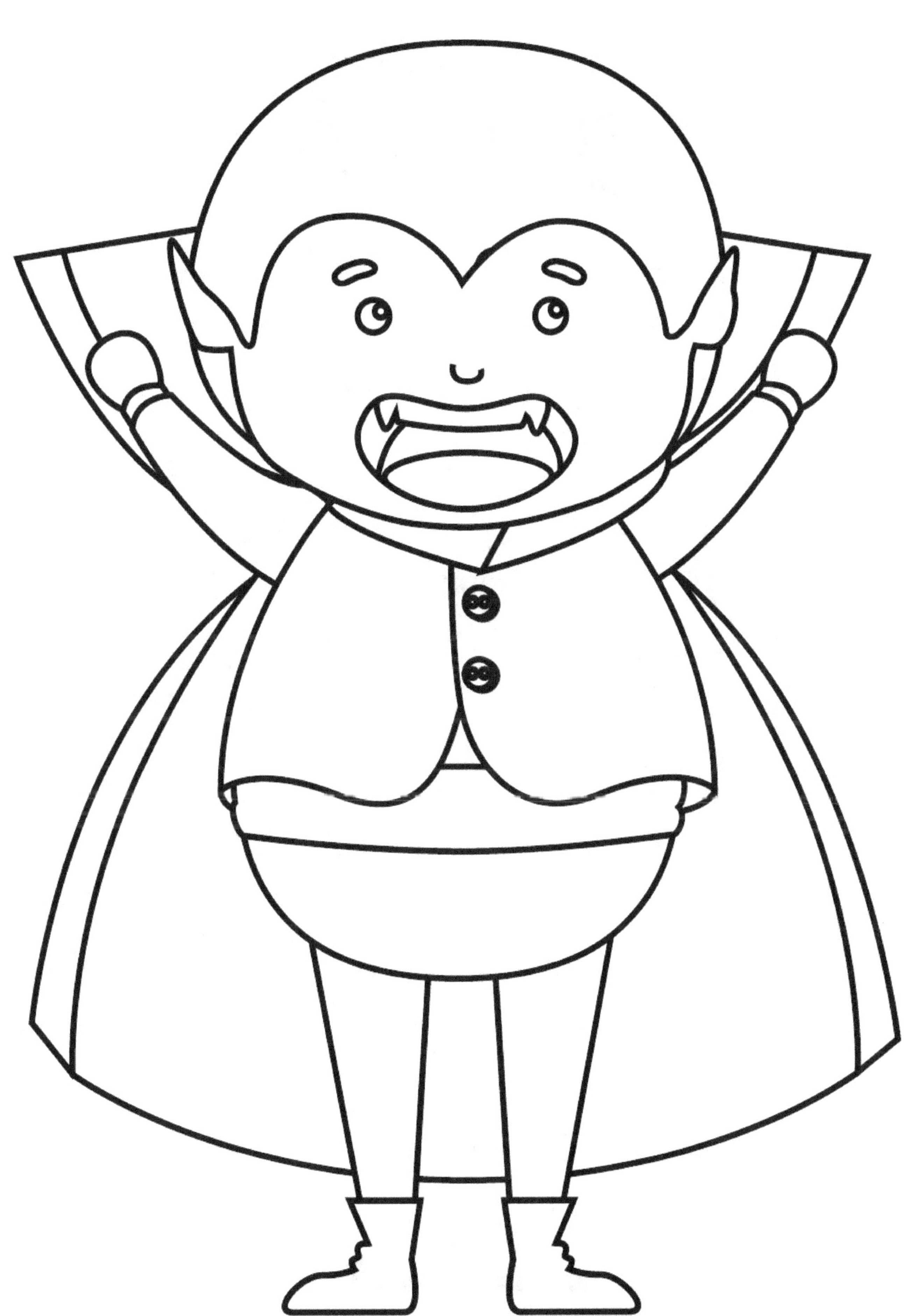

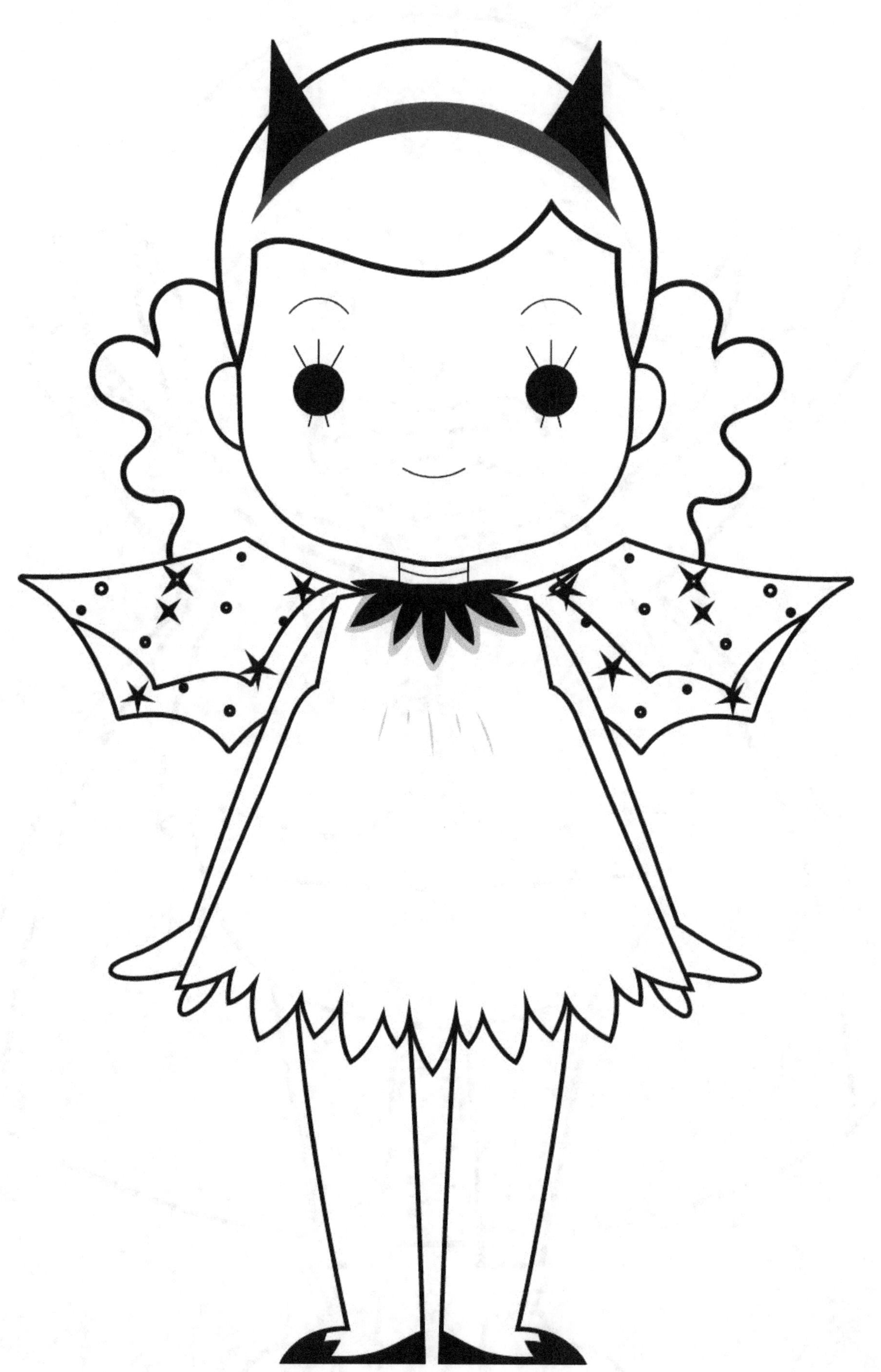

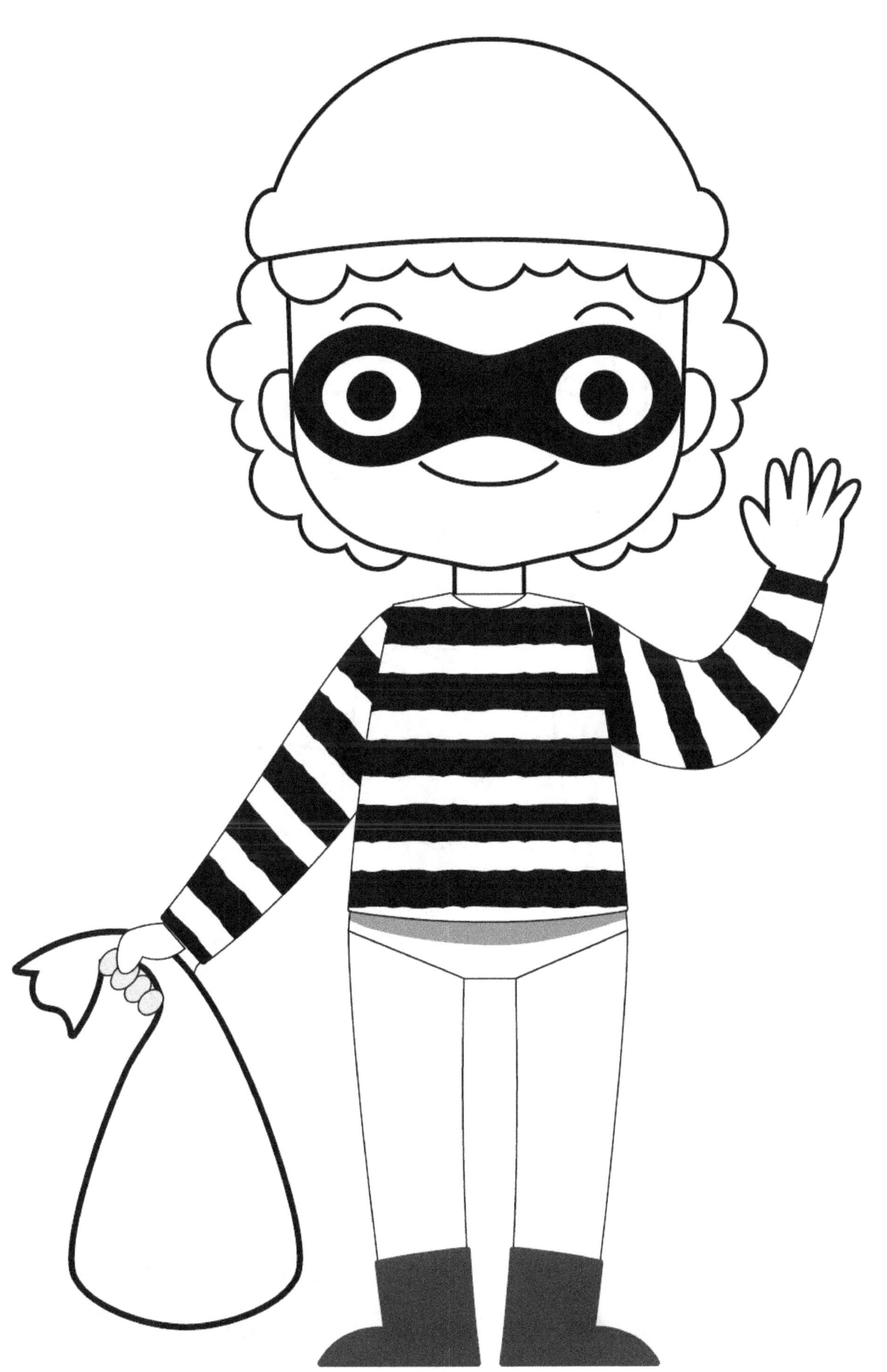

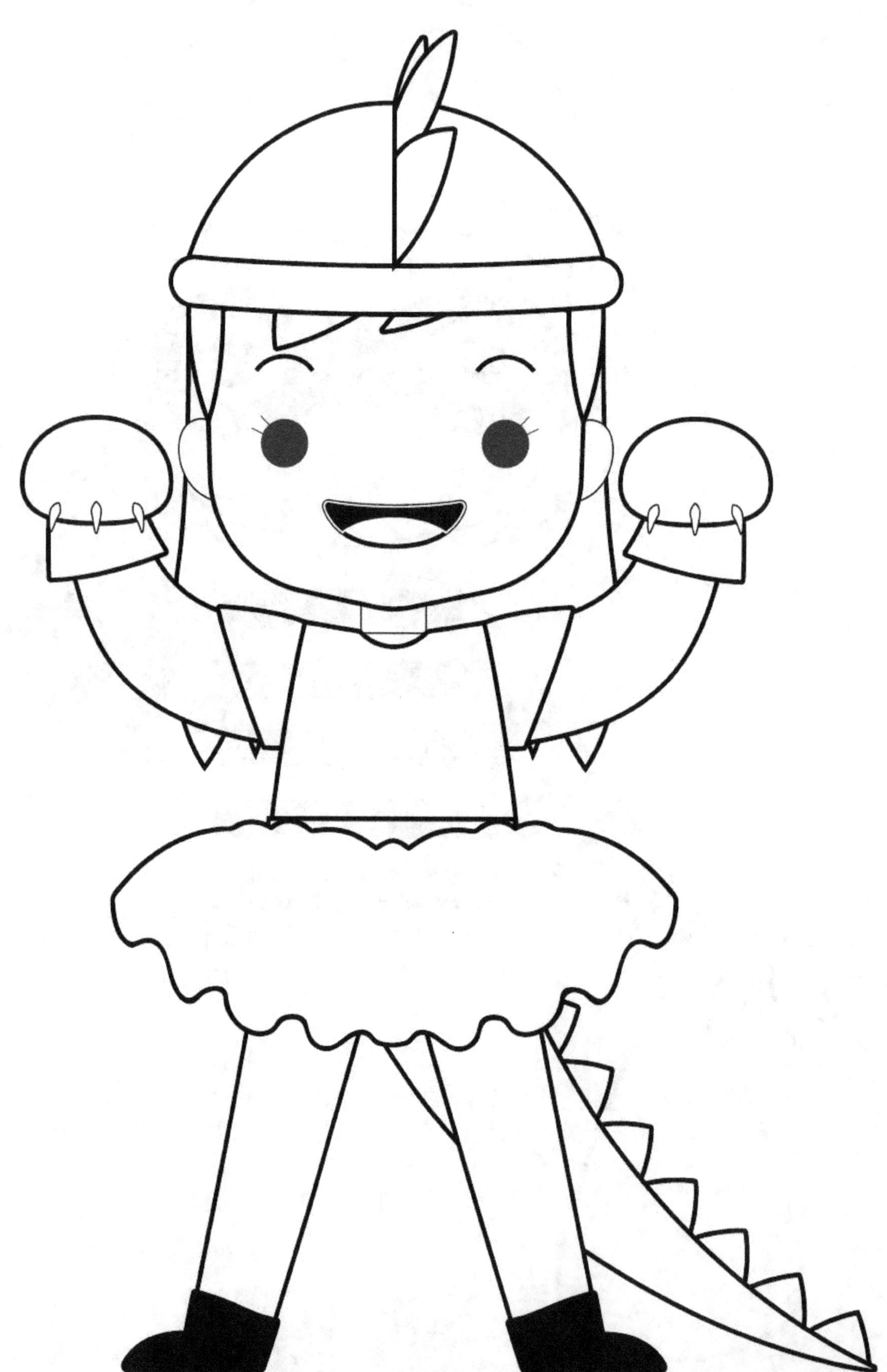

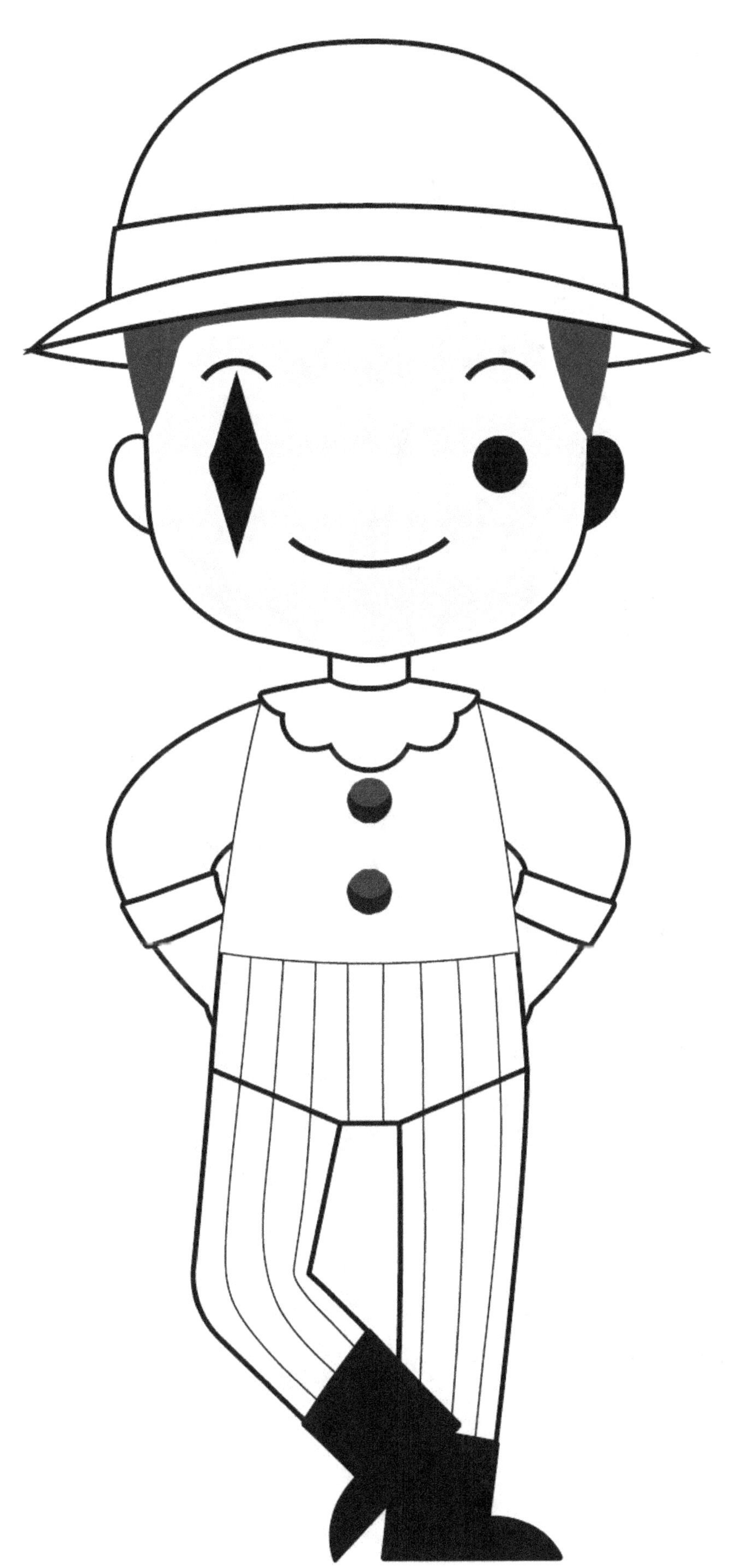

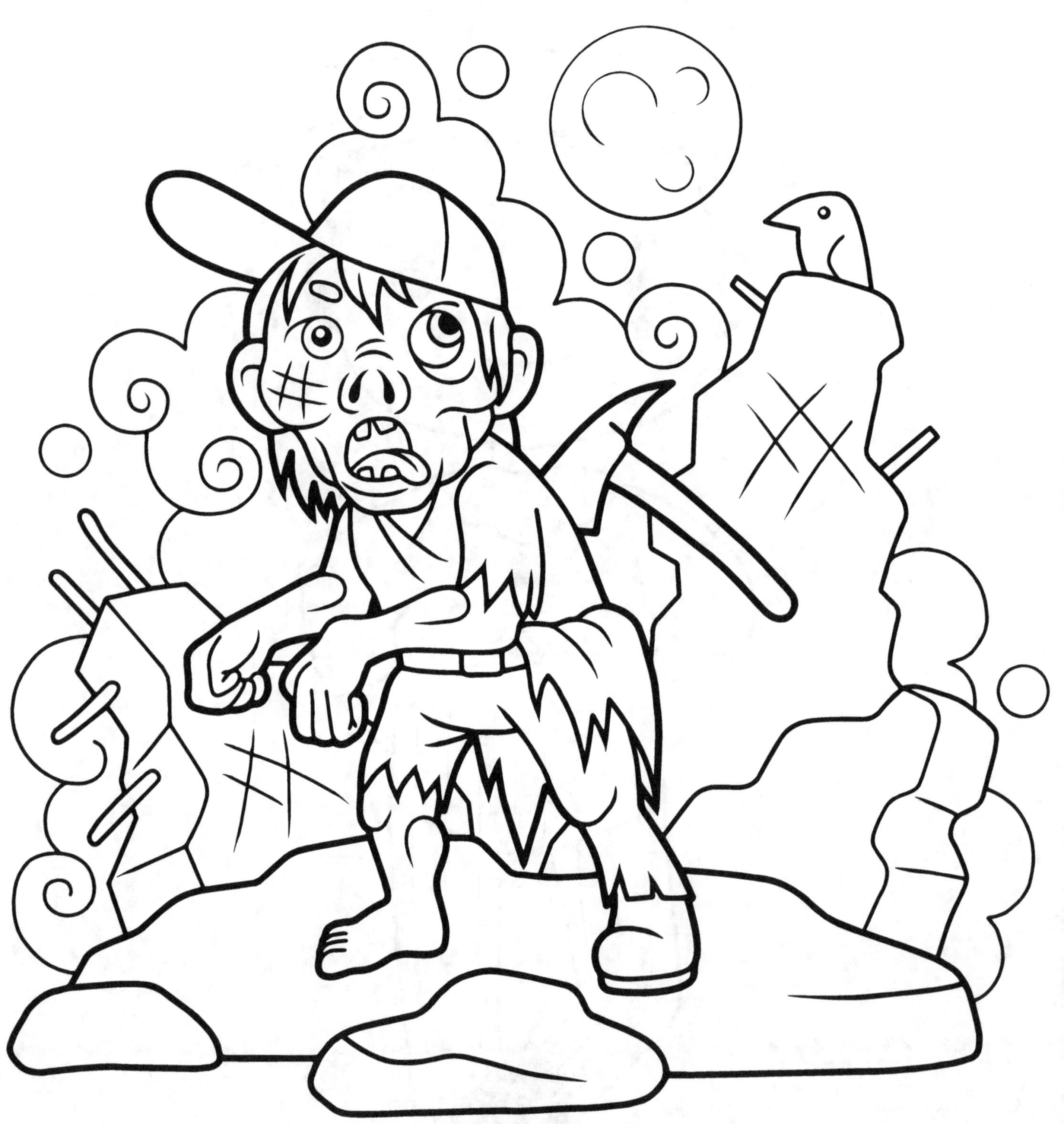

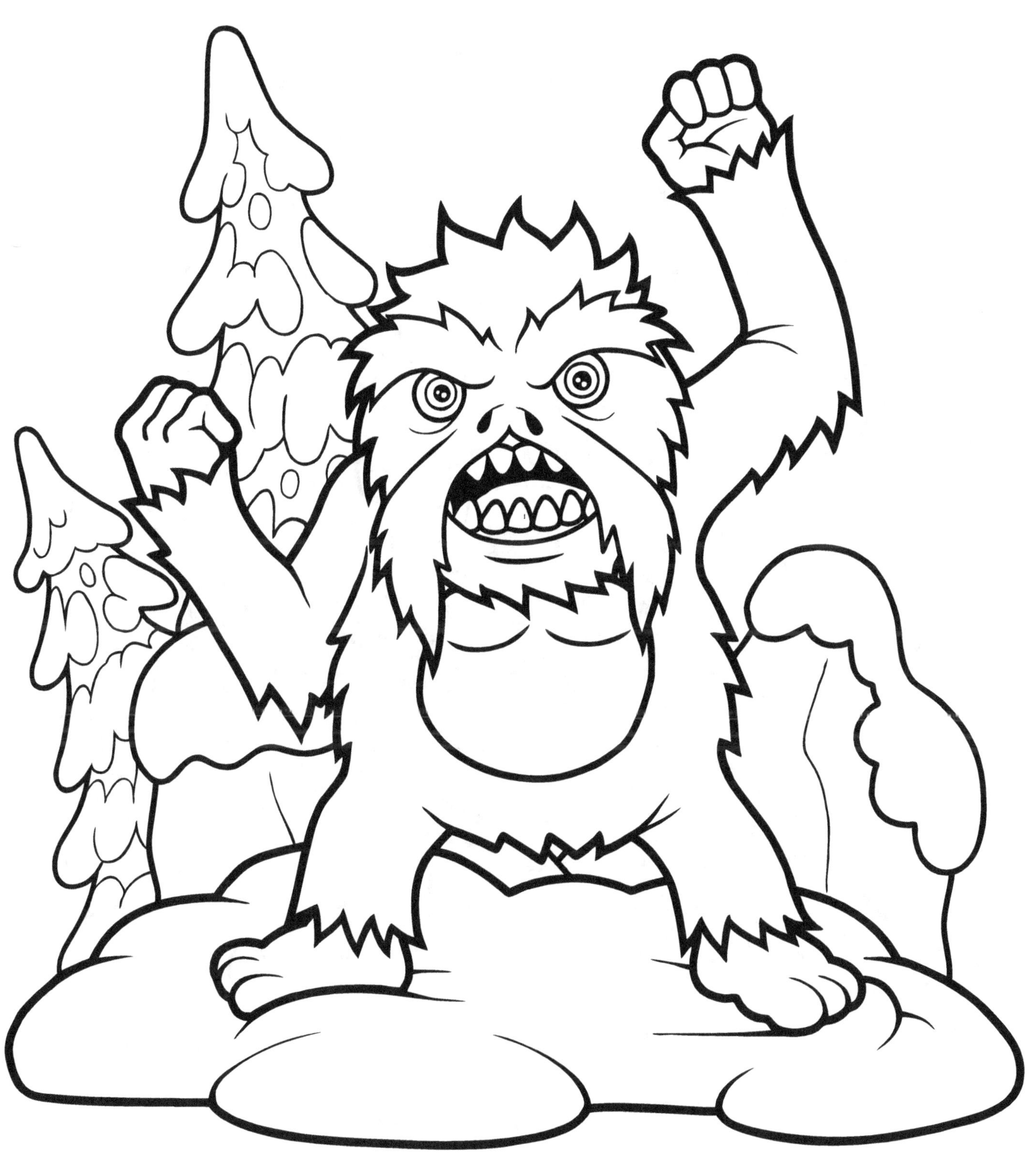

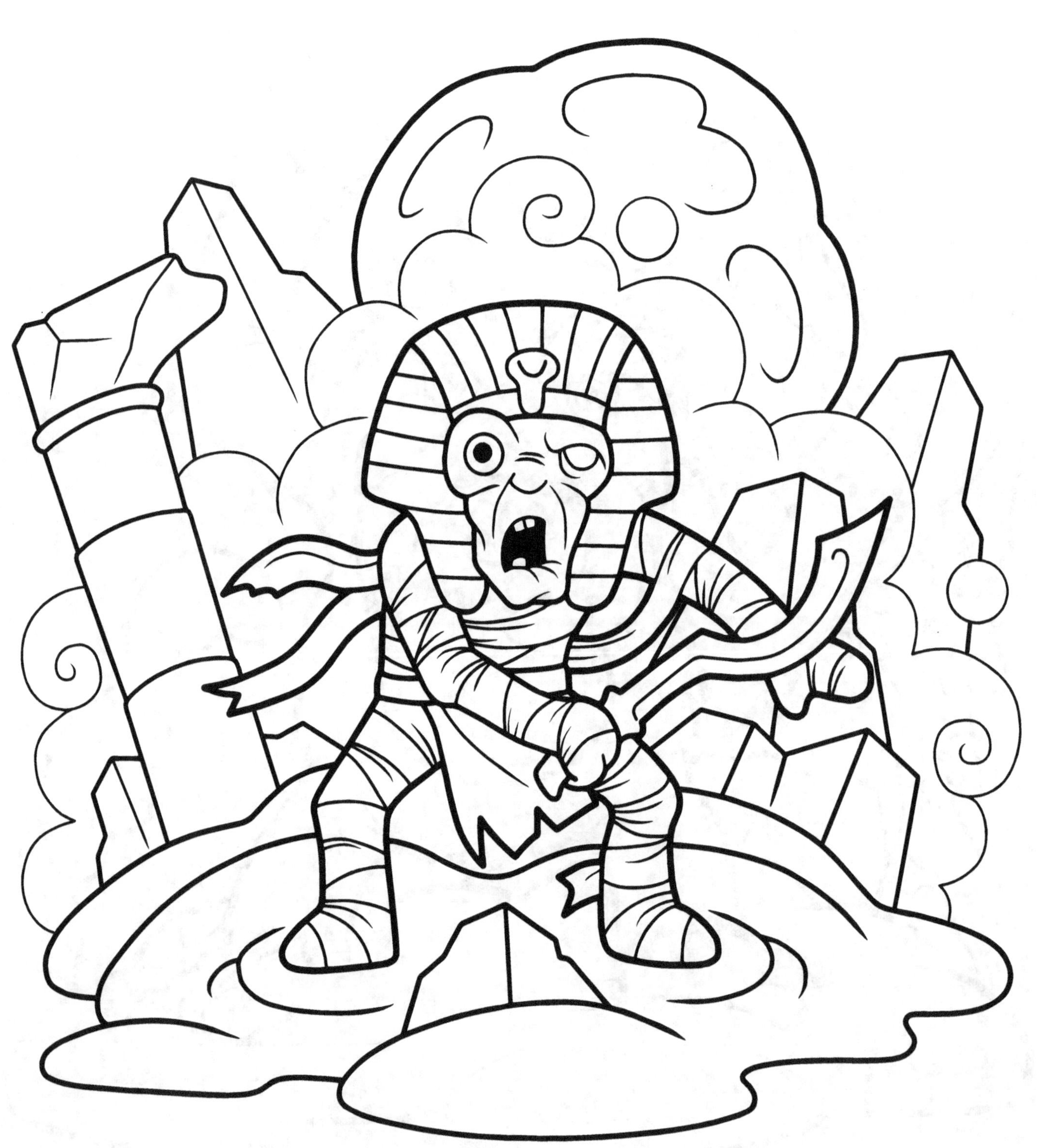

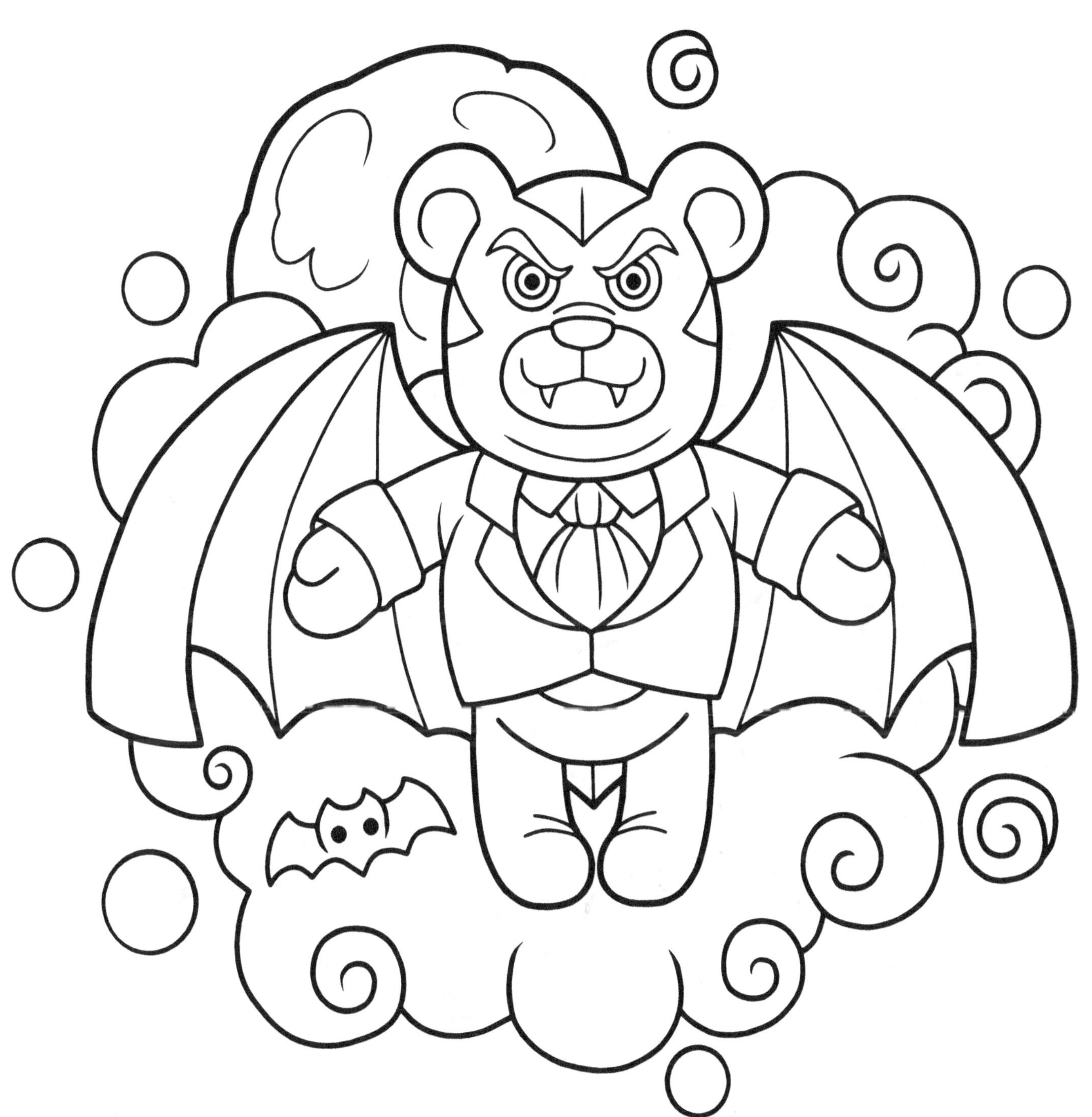

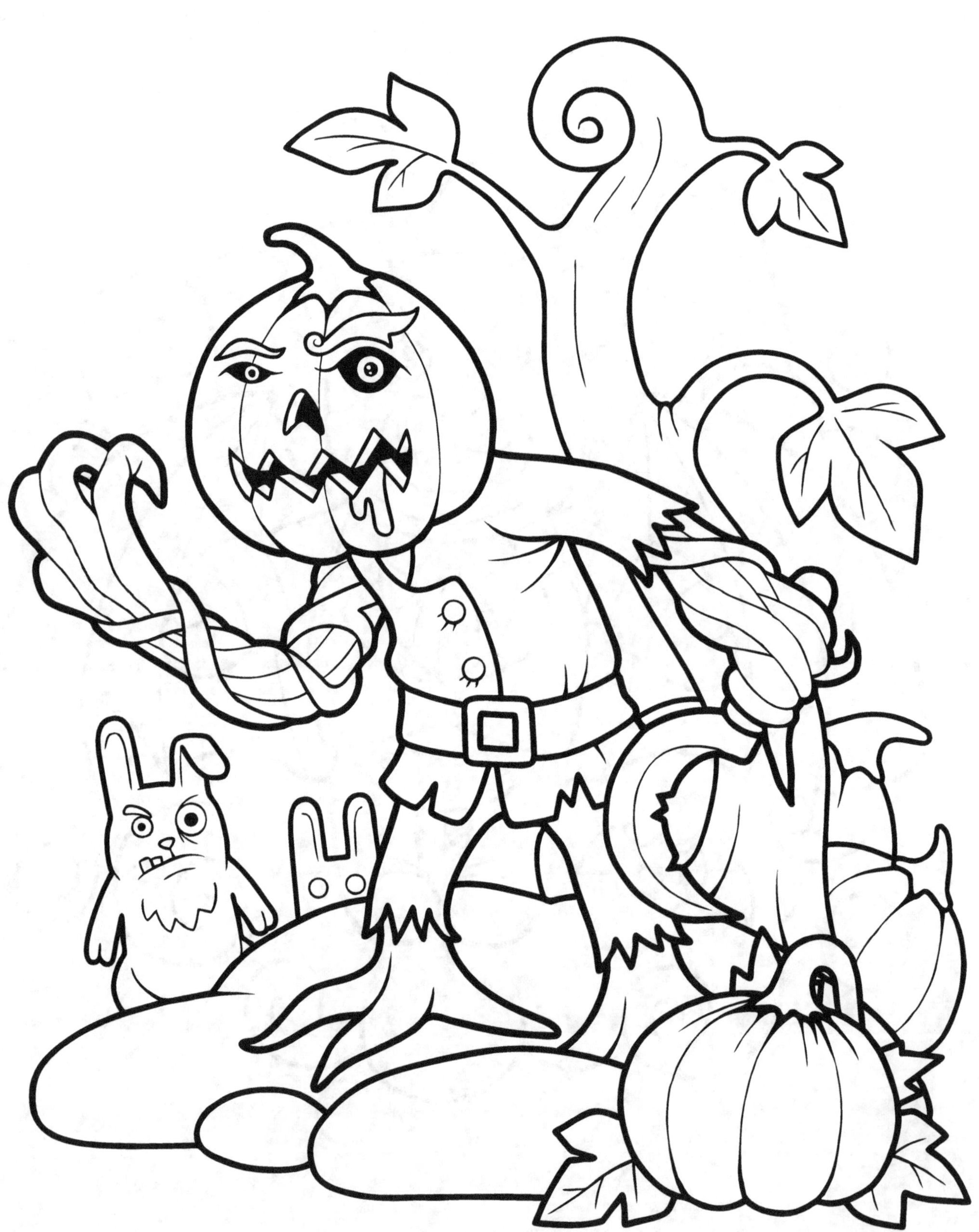

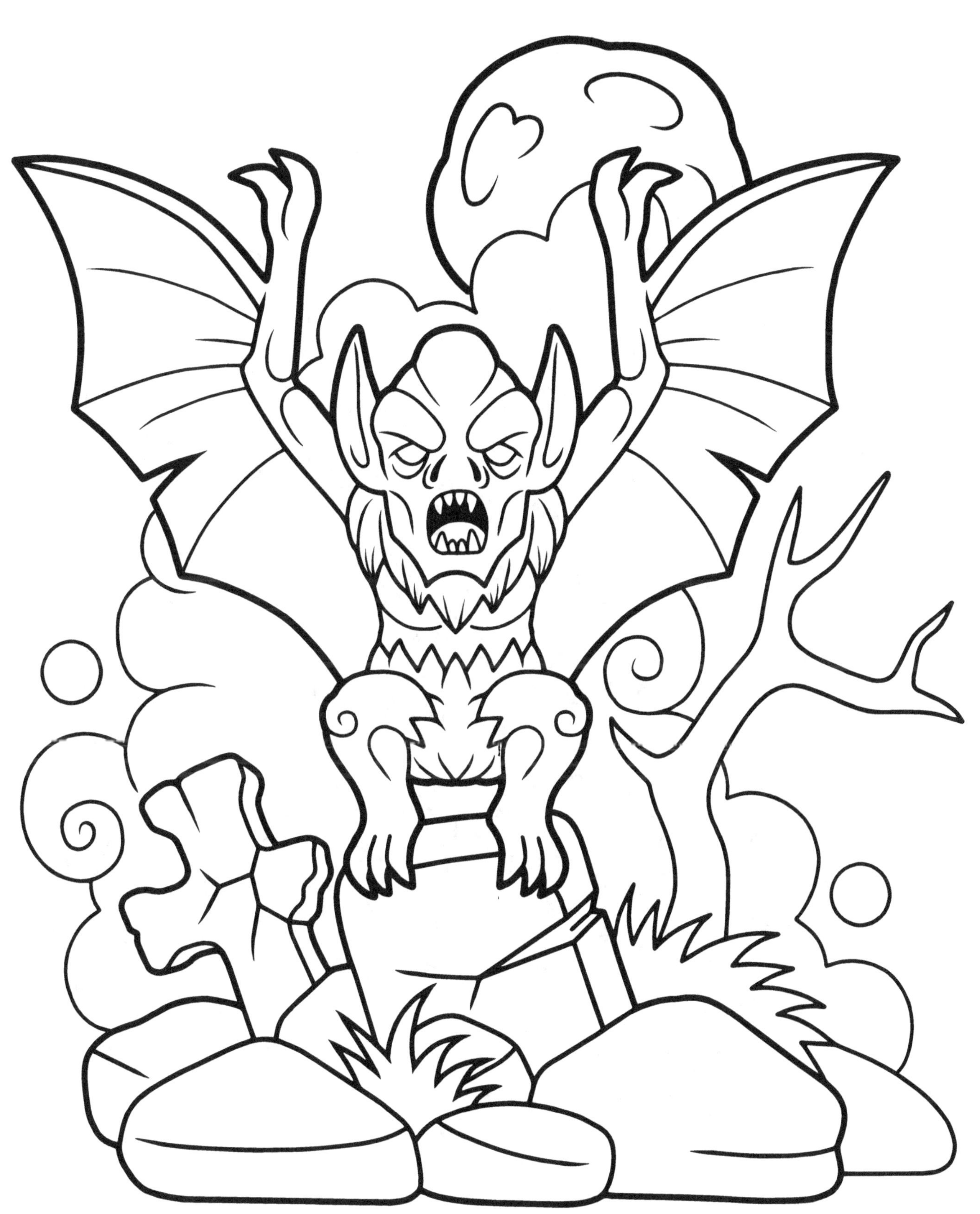

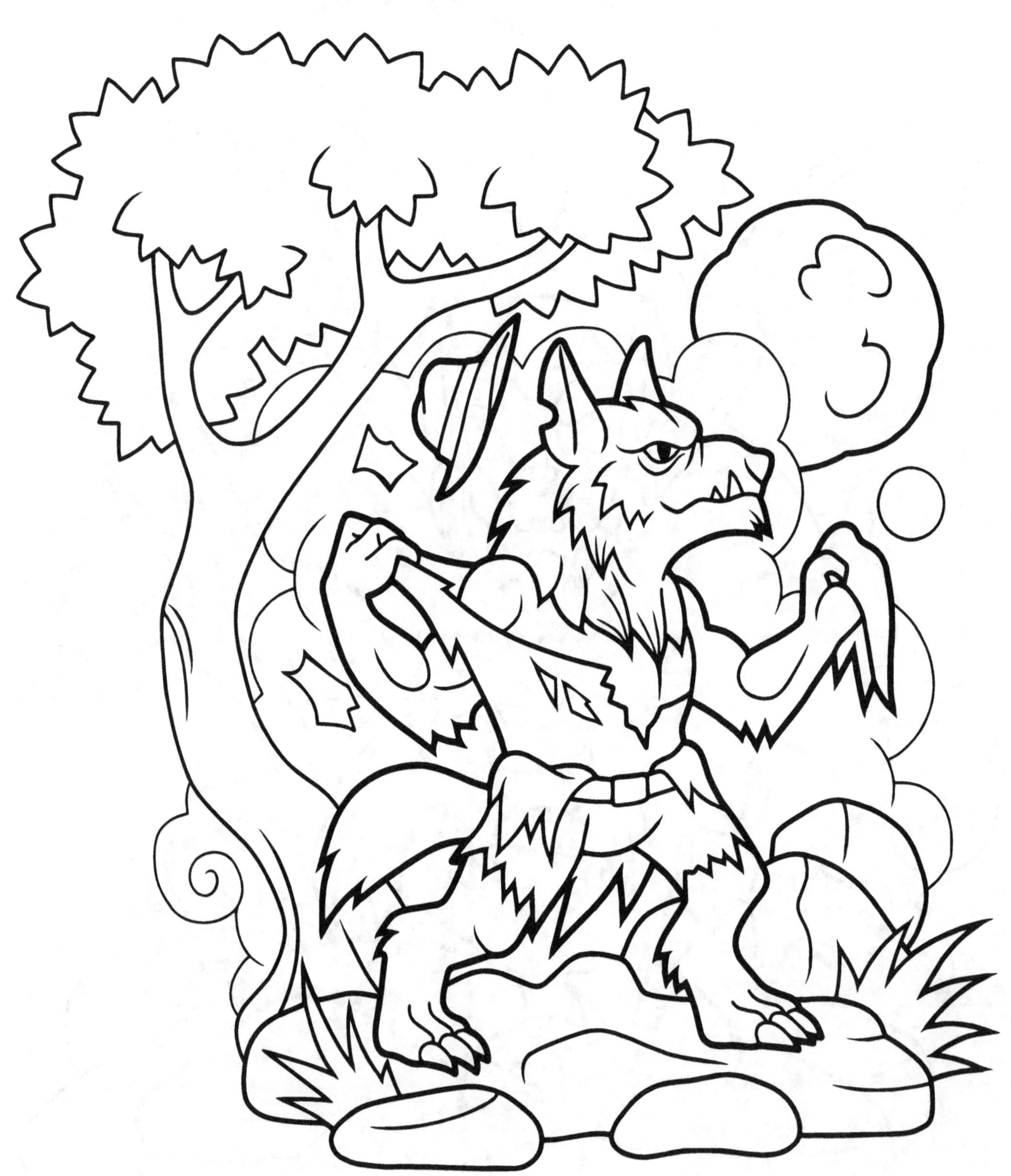

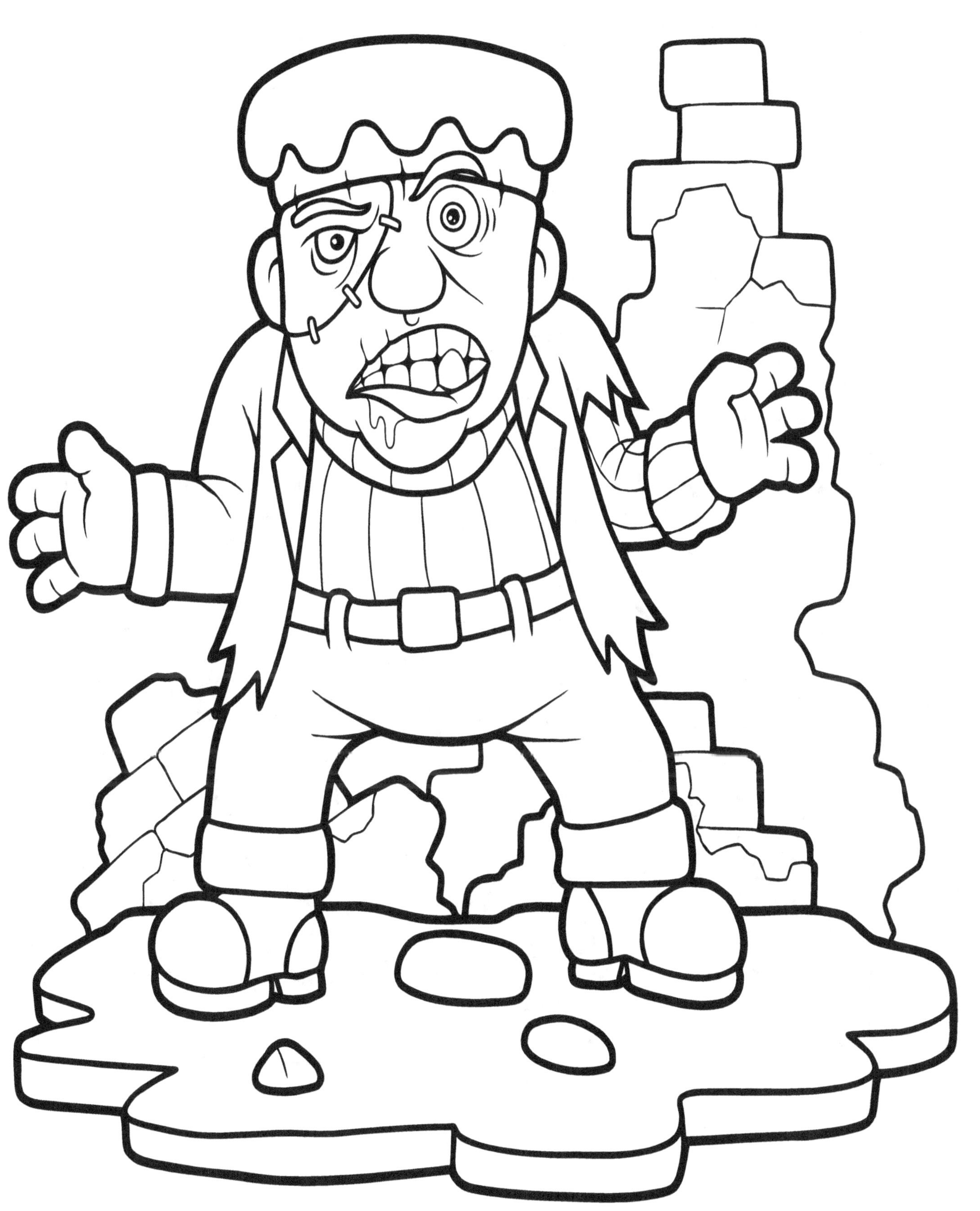

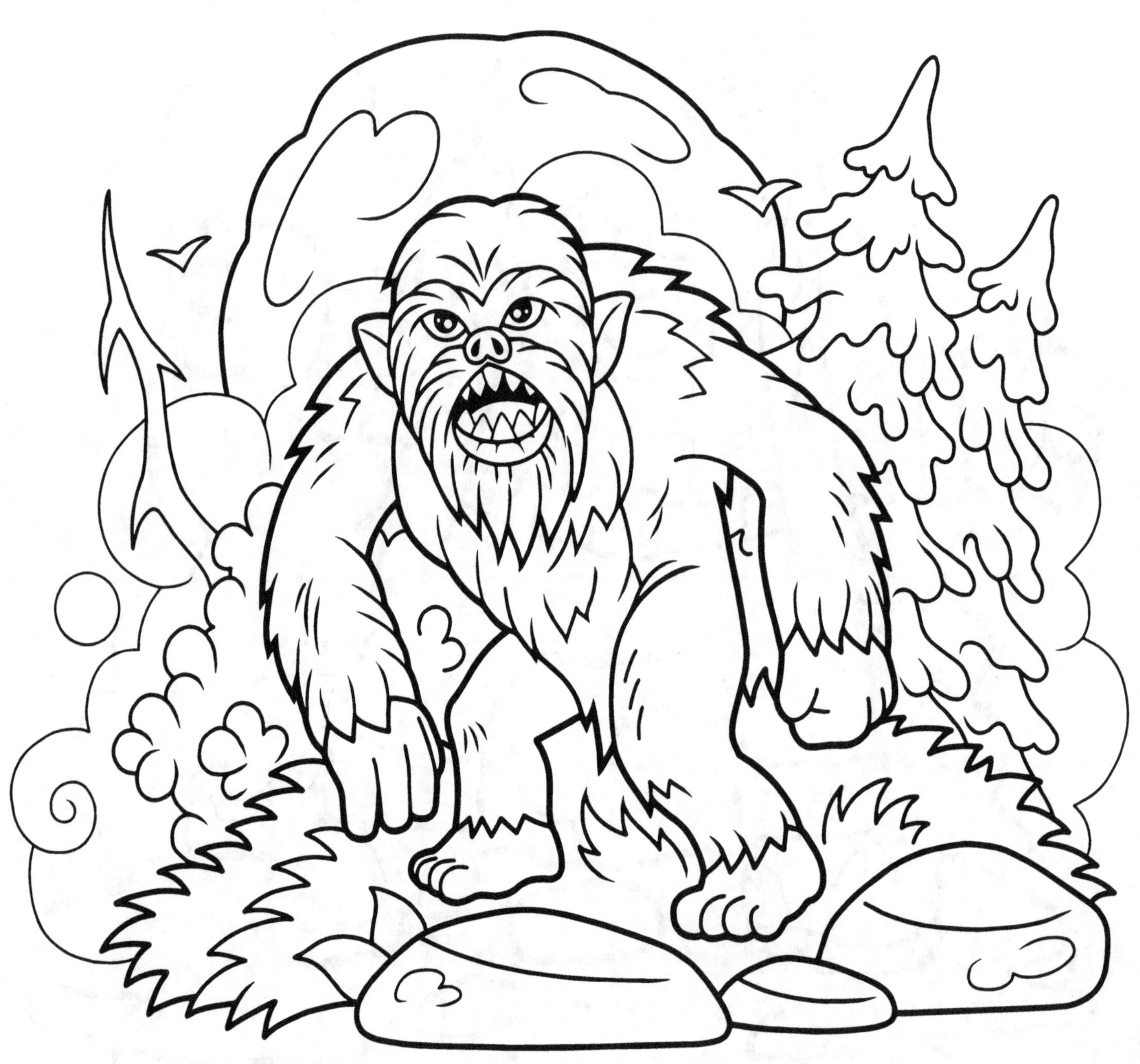

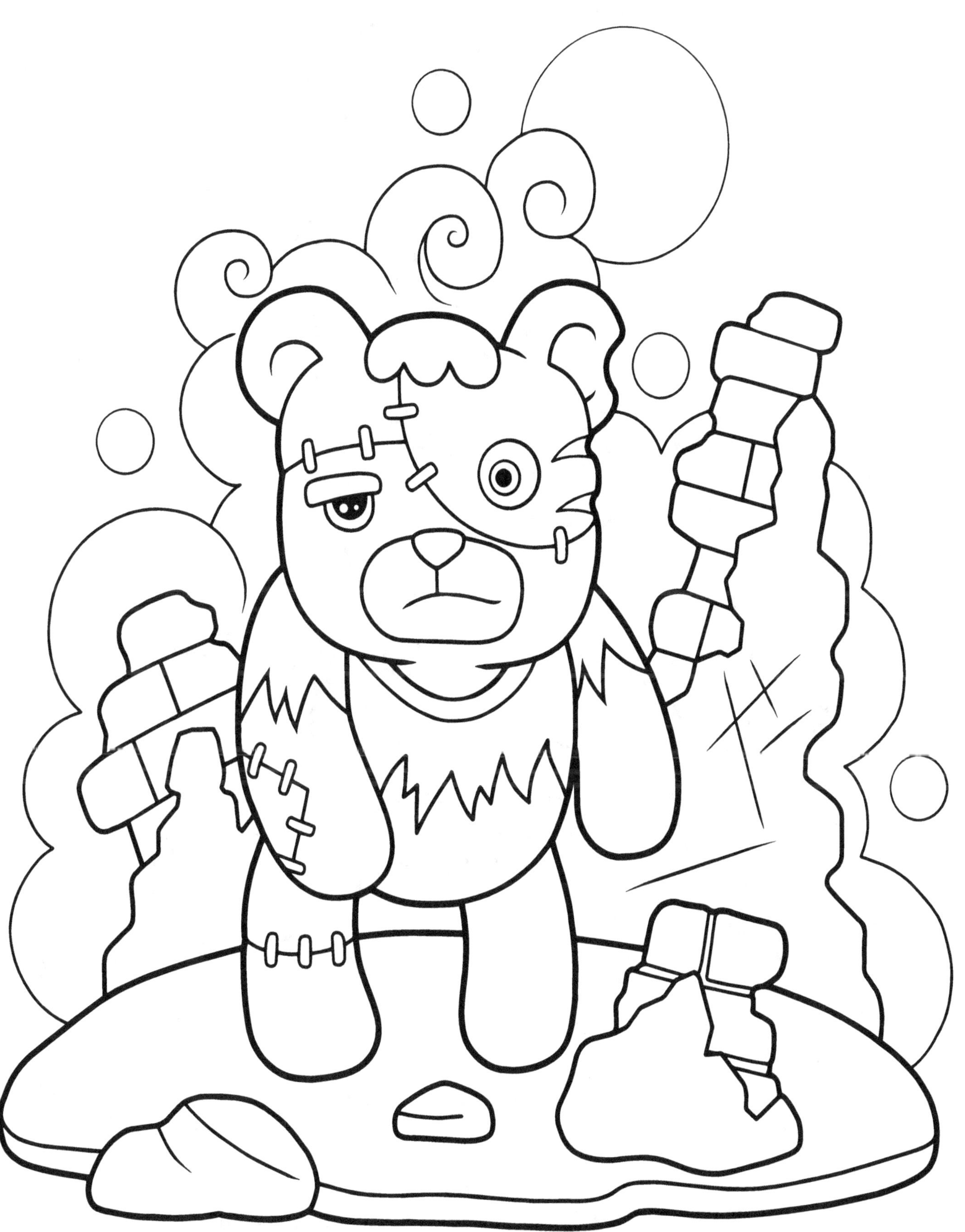

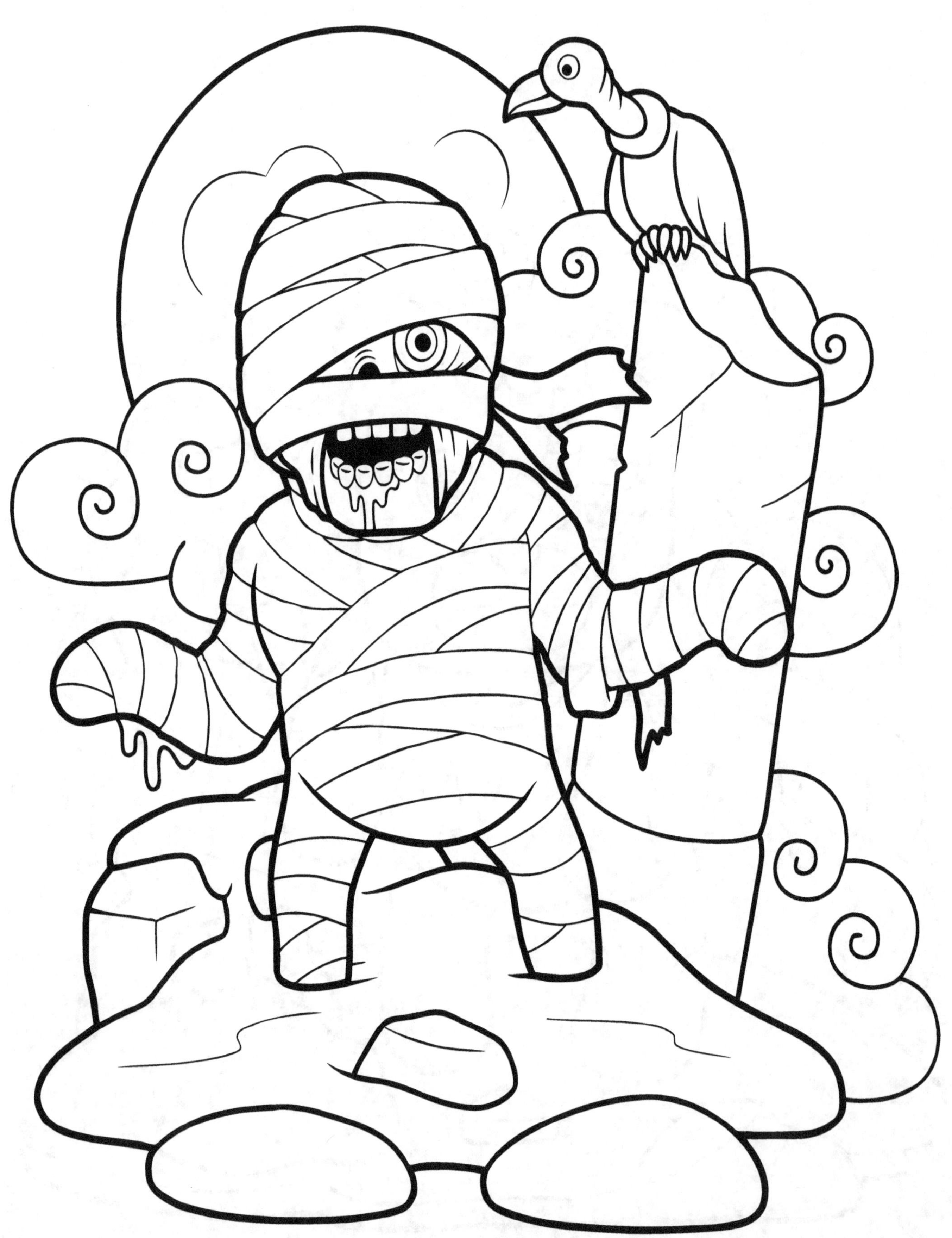

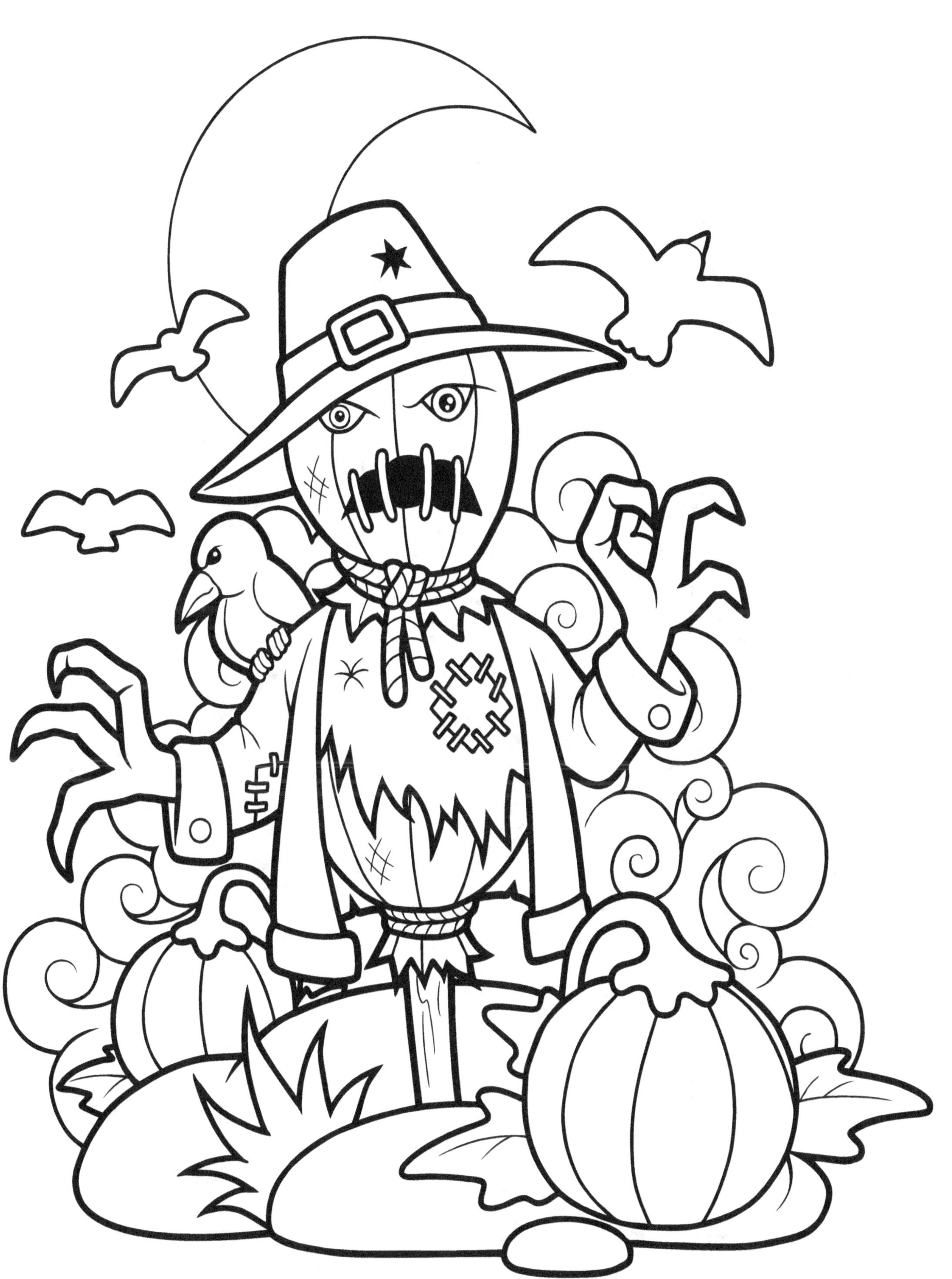

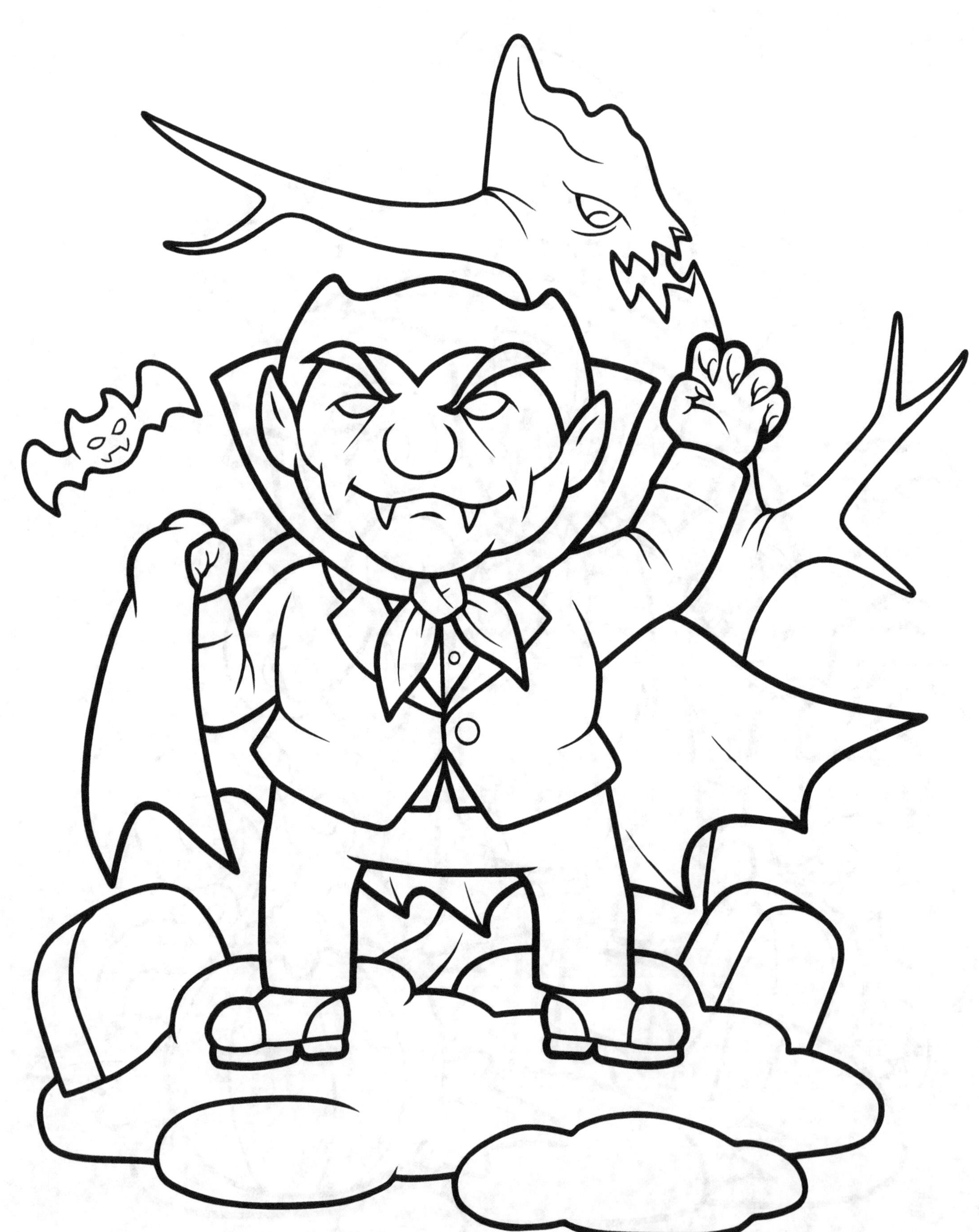

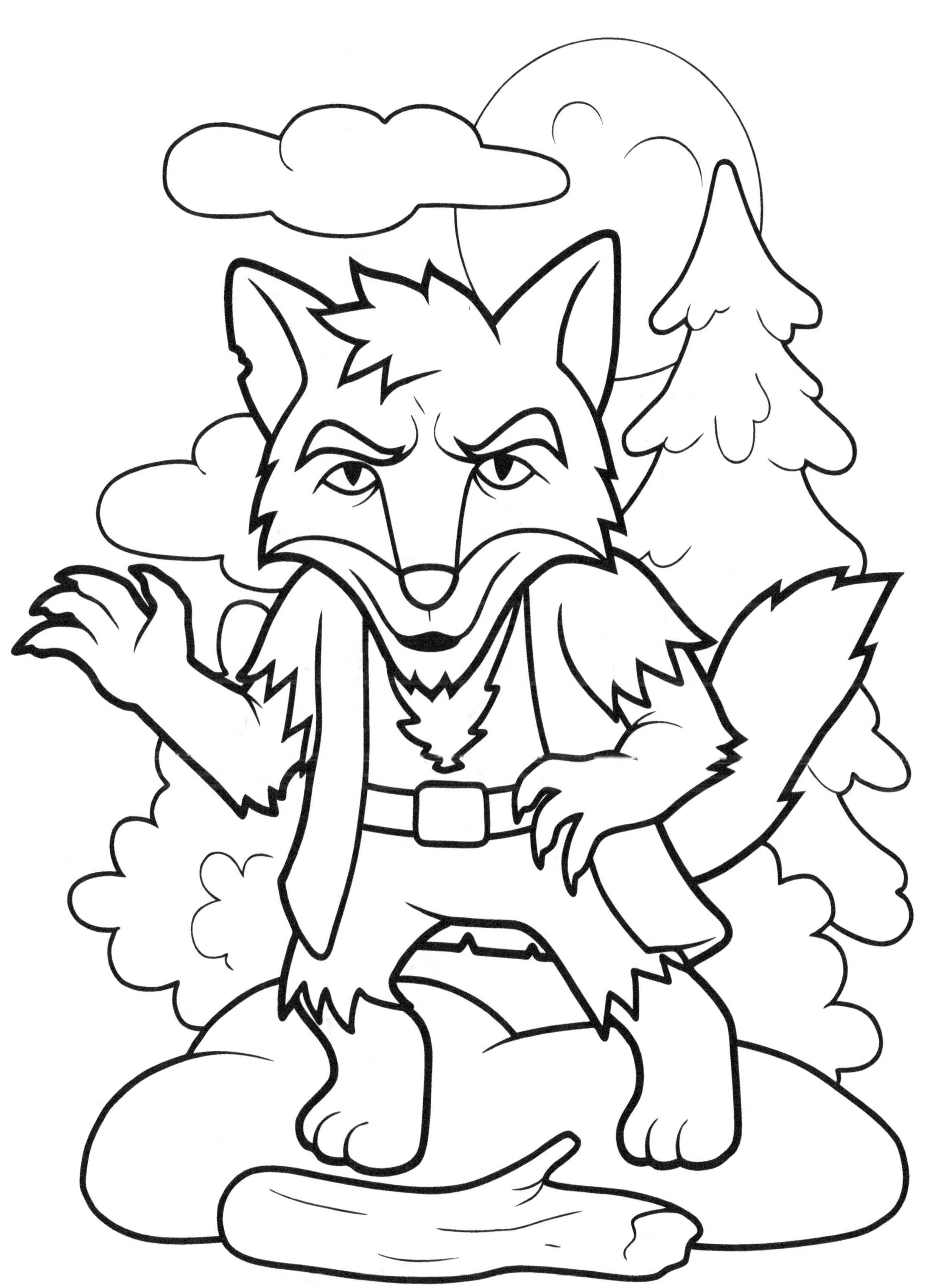

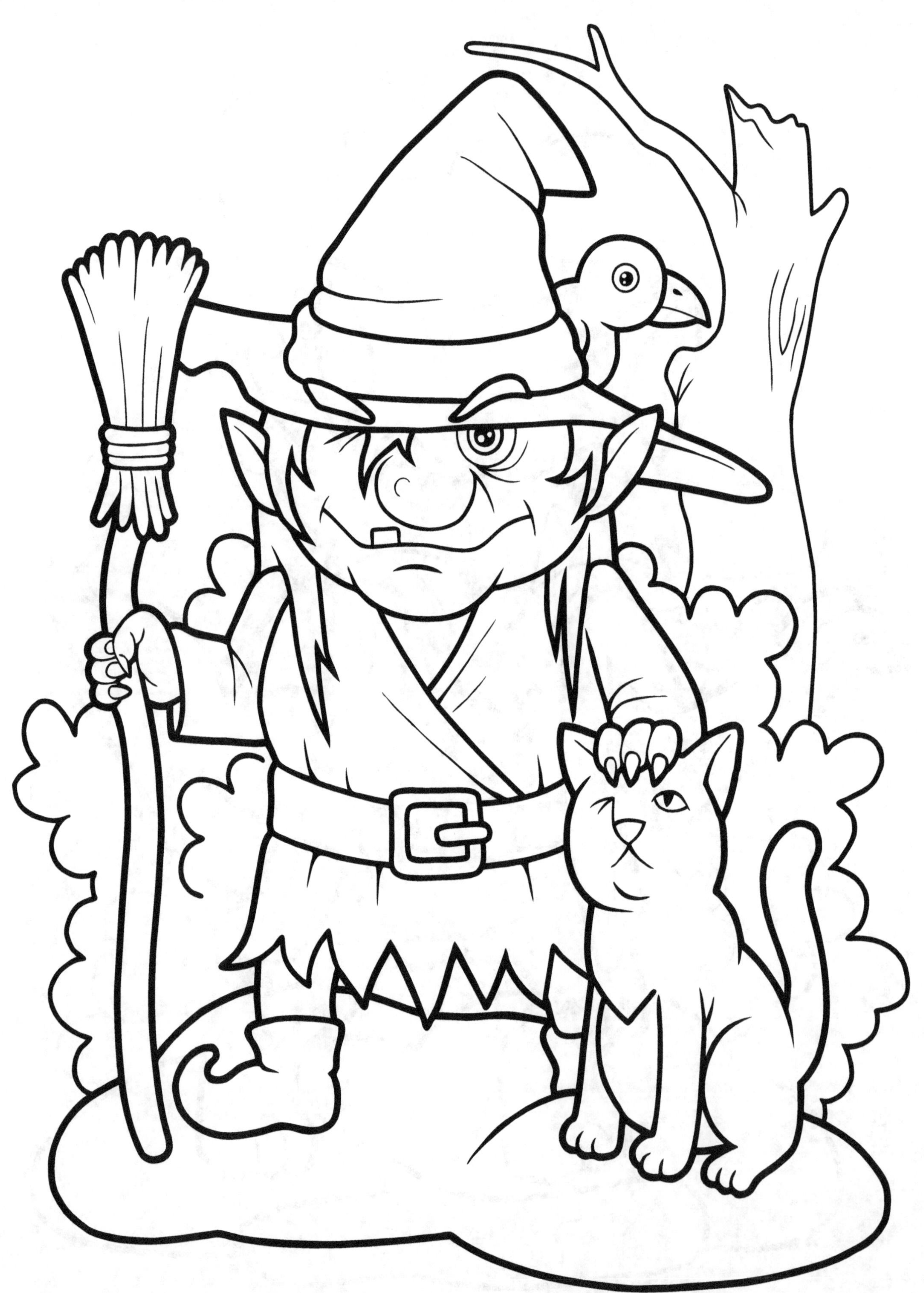

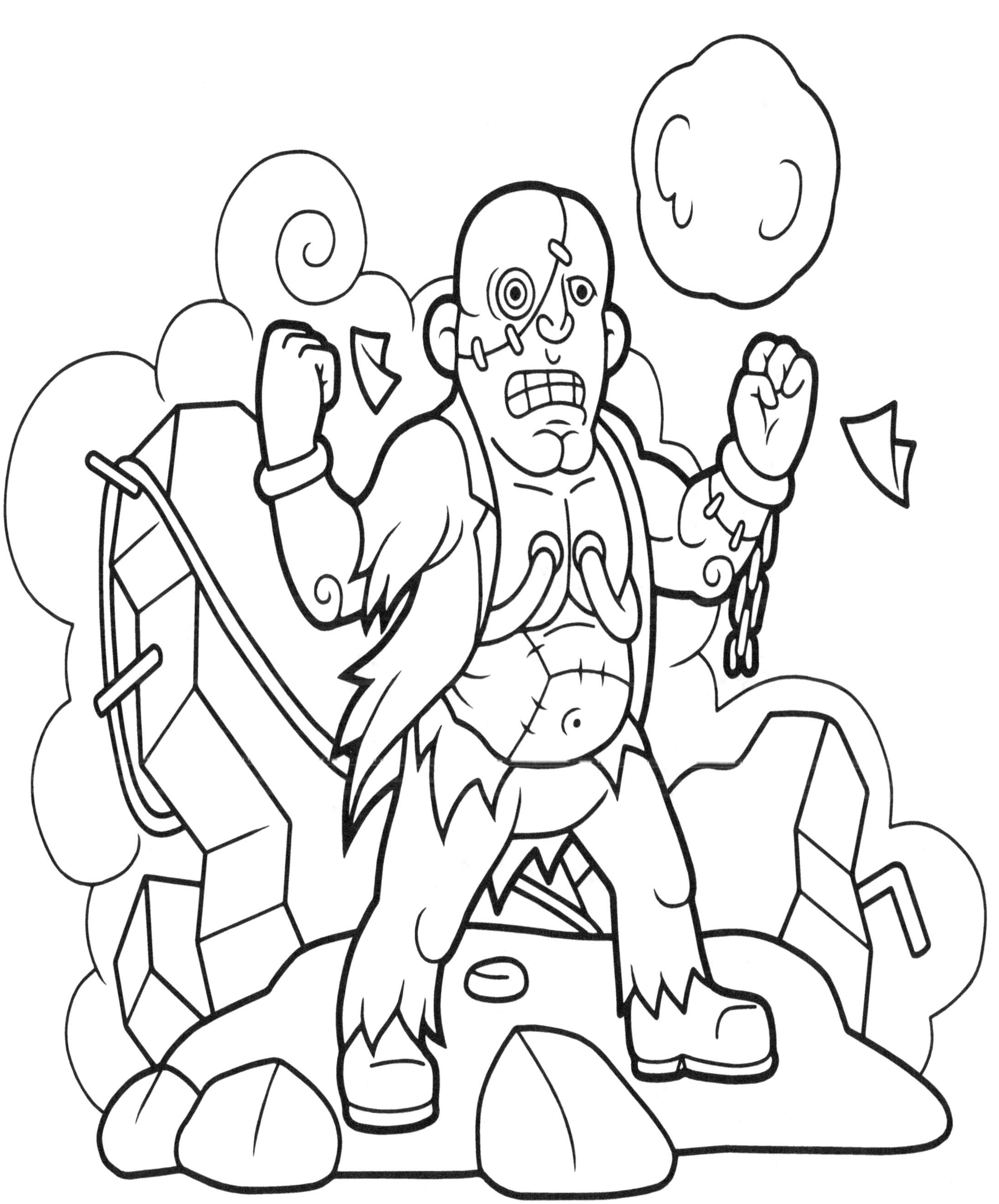

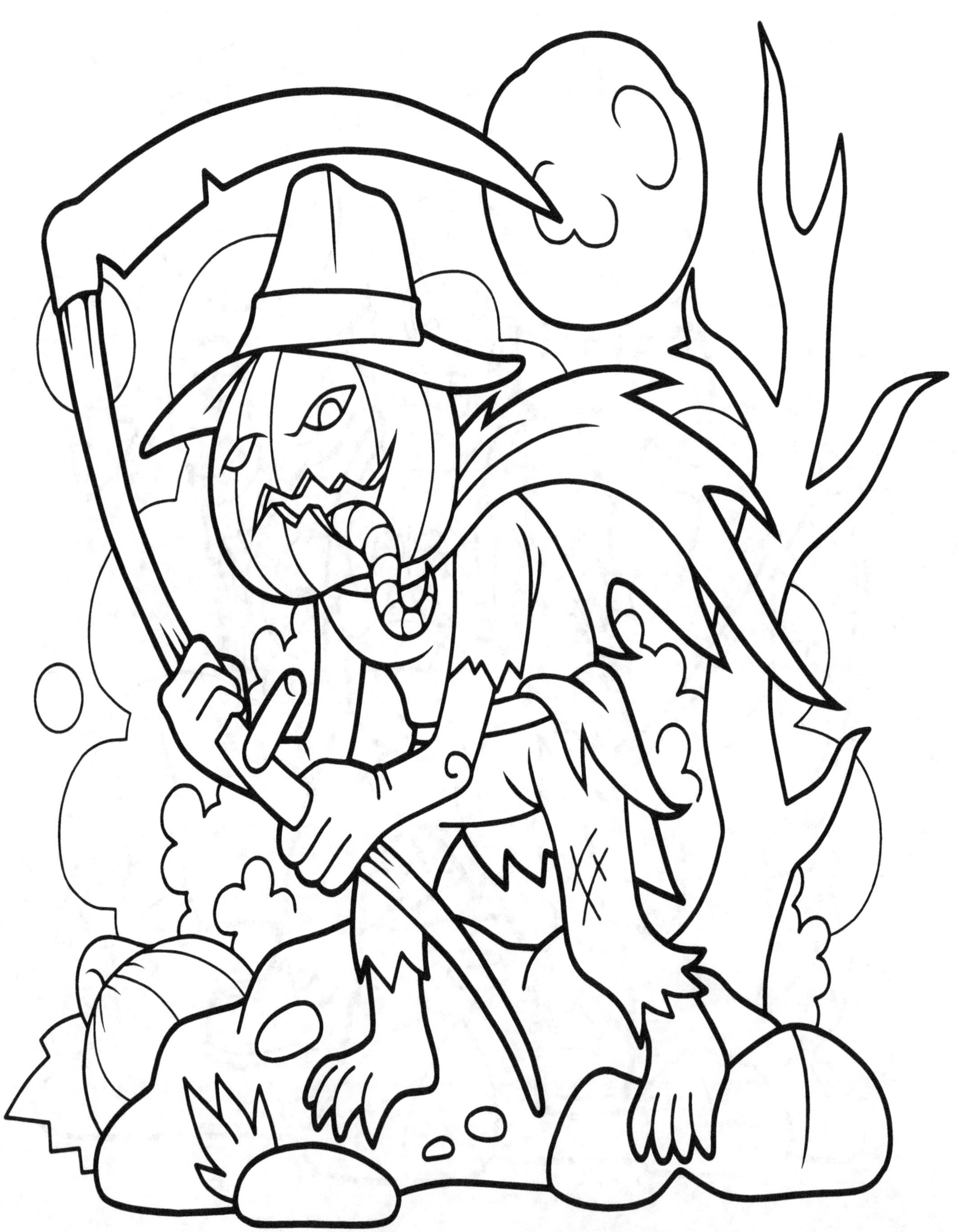

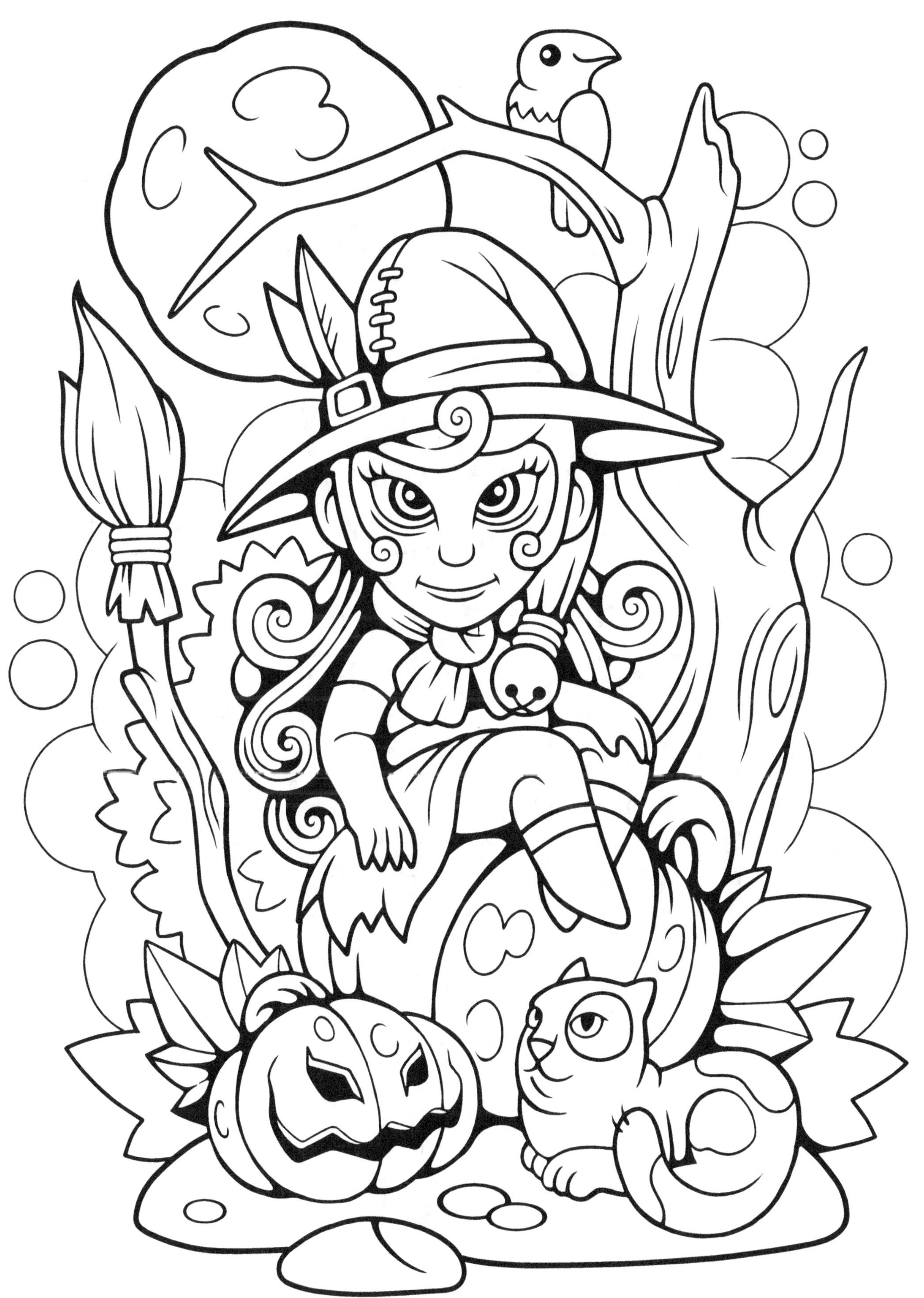

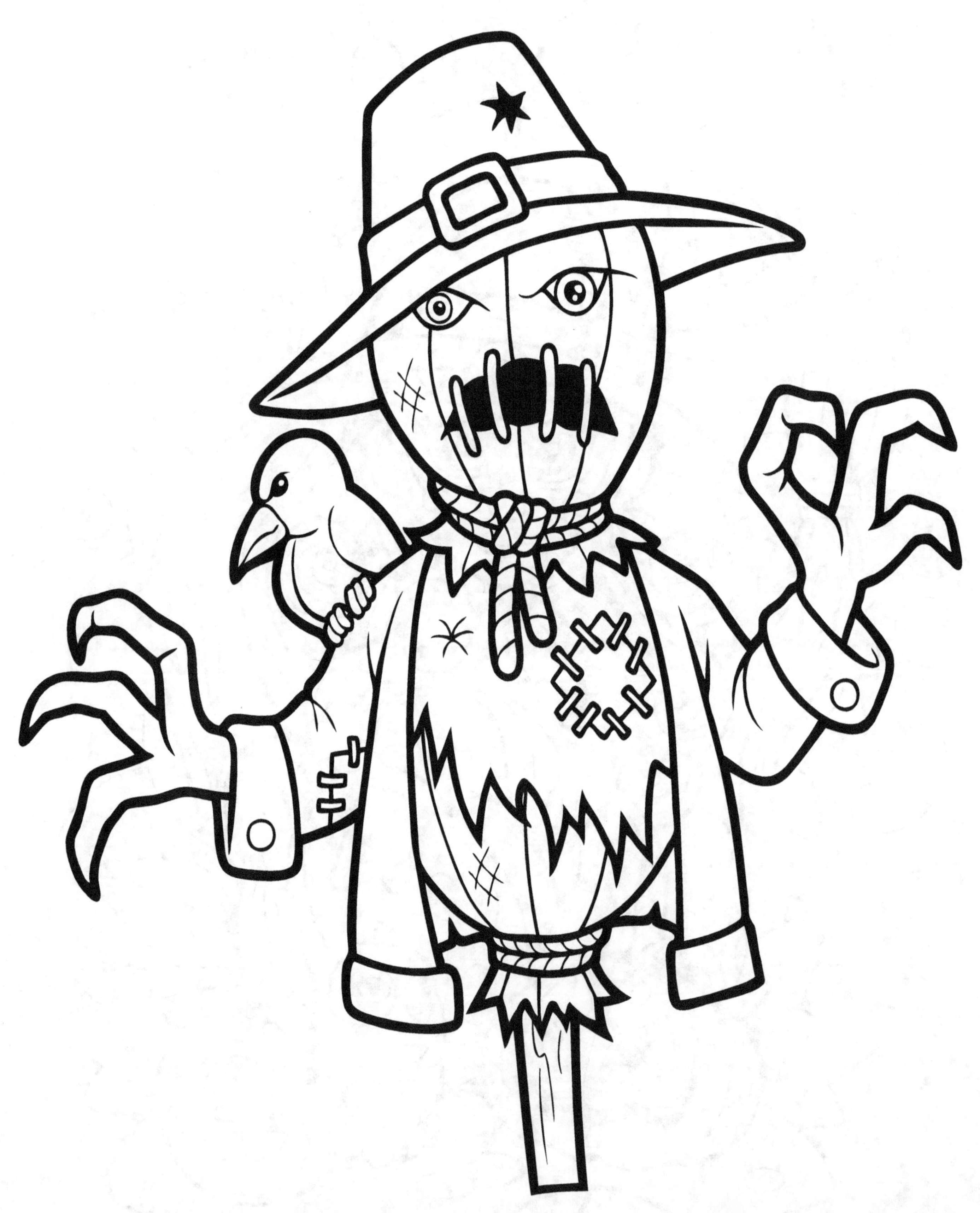

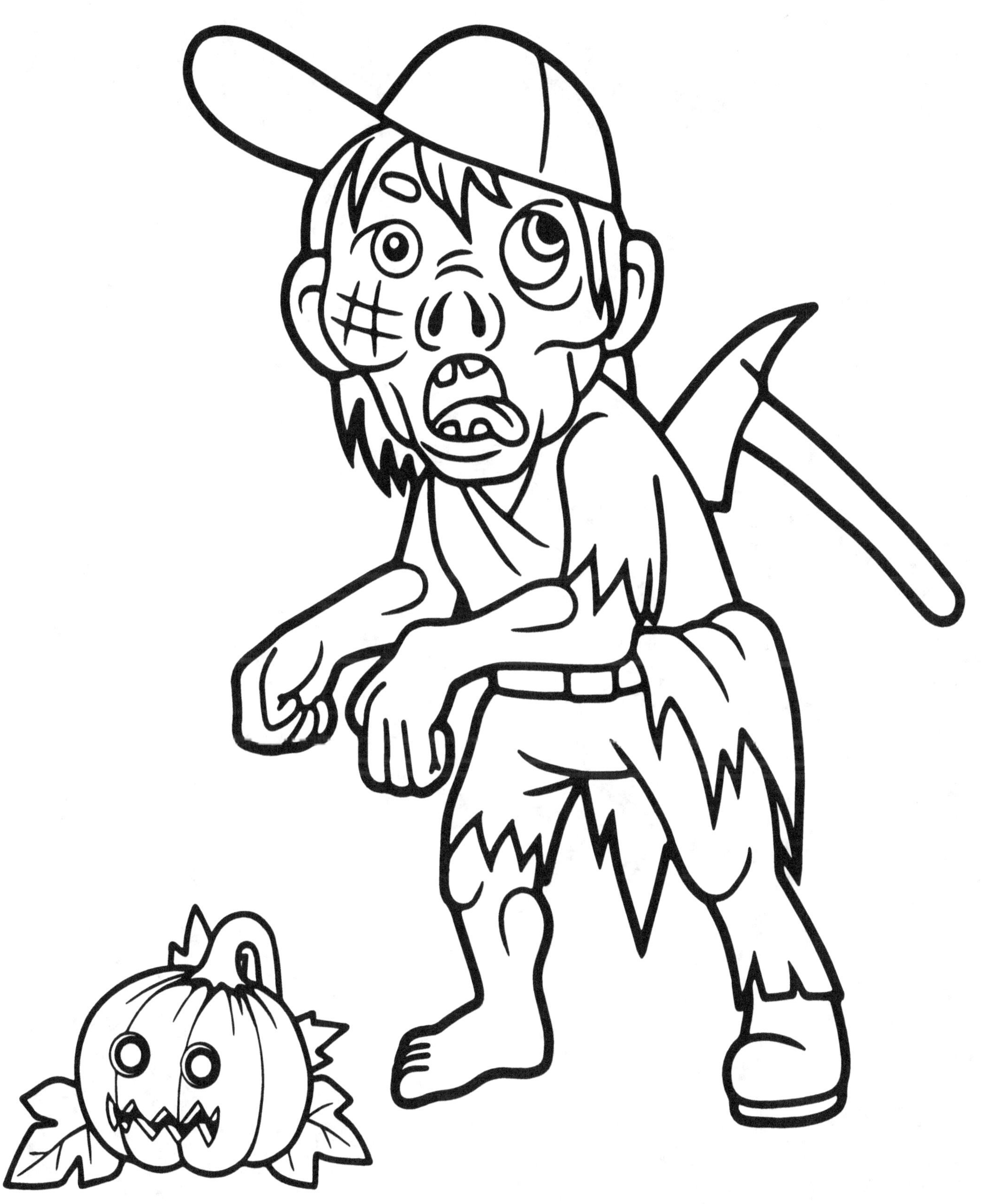

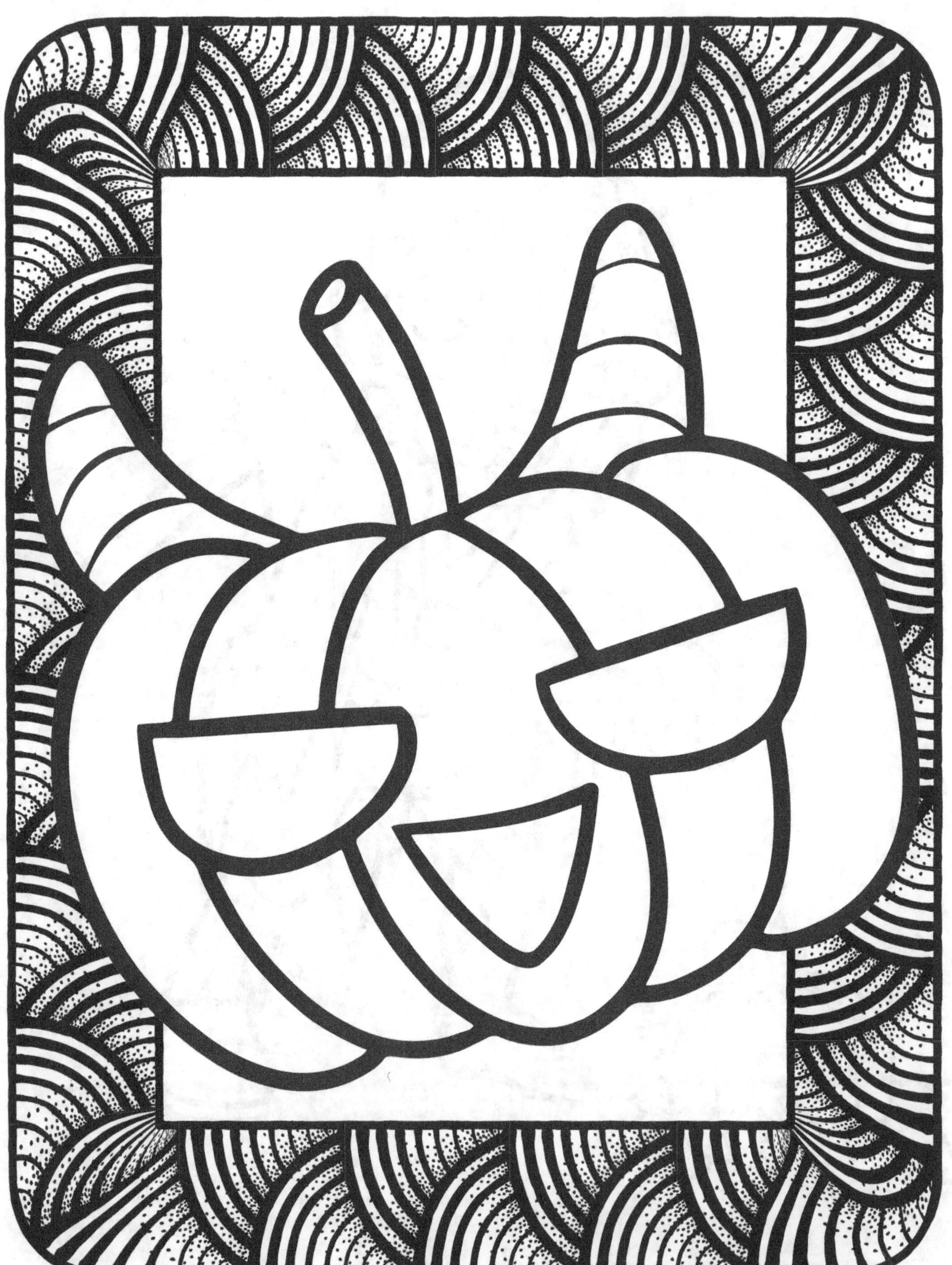

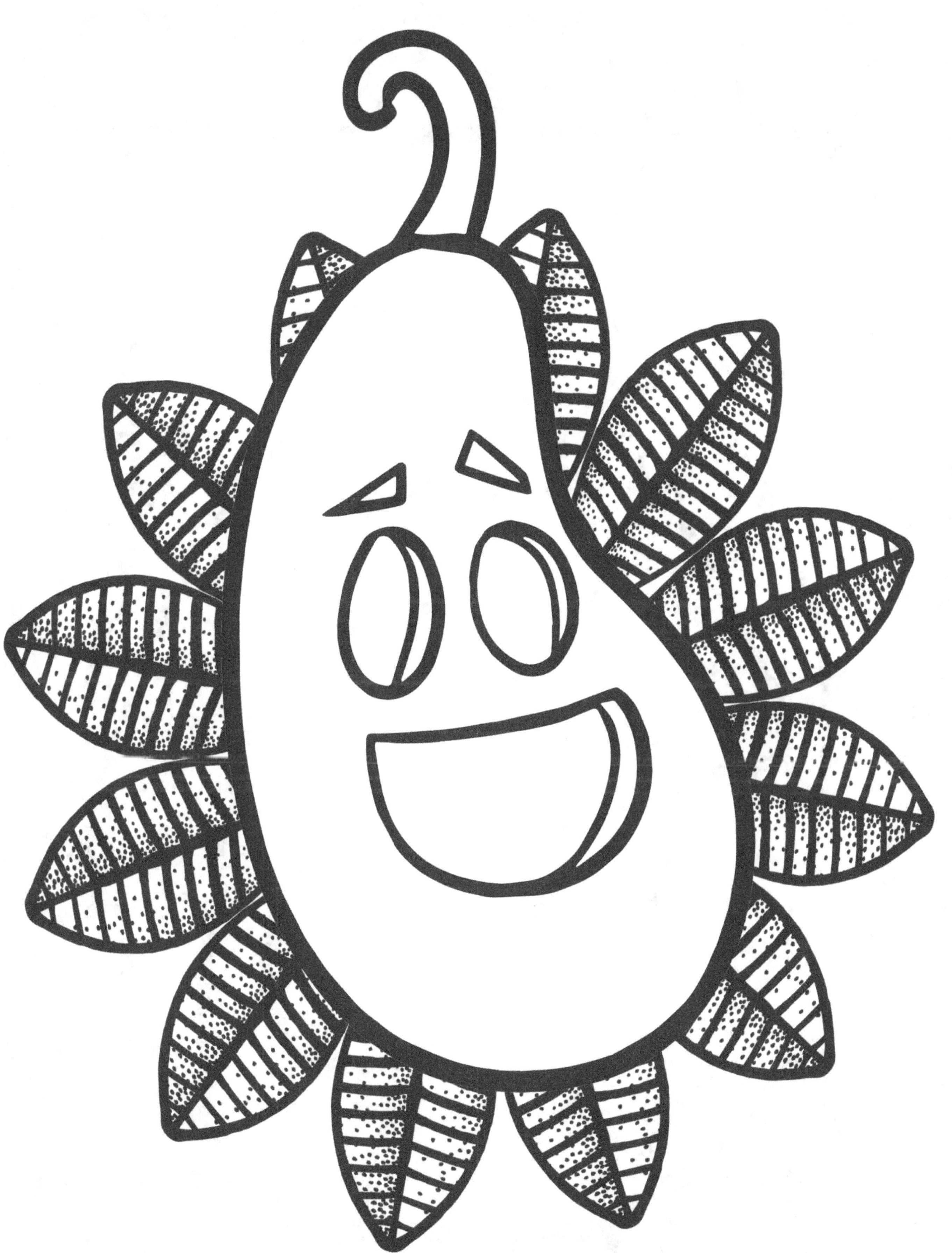

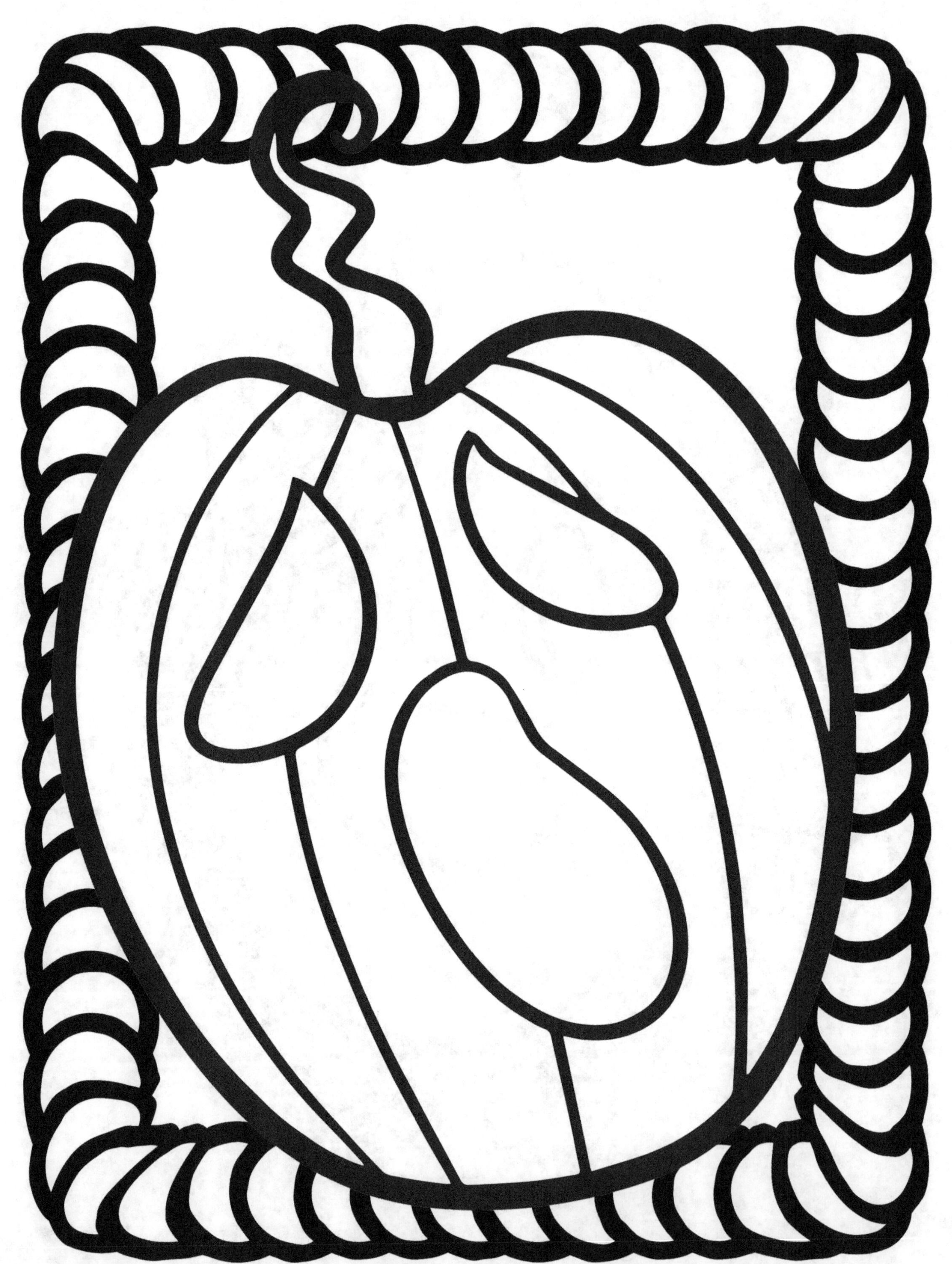